PRAISE FC

Disruptive Di

M000022316

We need to bring different voices to the table and leverage divergent thinking to truly explore various perspectives and generate many possibilities. Convergent thinking isn't going to get us there because it's linear and going through a list of steps to get to a single answer rarely leads to innovation. Disruptive Discovery *can be a catalyst to get everyone involved on the divergent thinking path.*

—Kay Sargent, Senior Principal, HOK

Finally! Someone has taken the abused term "discovery"—used so often in the wrong way by salespeople—and given it the attention—and sorting—that it so desperately needed. In Disruptive Discovery, *Geoff Snavely not only clearly and concisely captures every important point on the subject but gives readers the tactical steps that it takes to become an expert at this important sales skill. A must-read for every sales professional.*

—Tom Snyder, Founder and Managing Partner, Funnel Clarity, LLC

If you're thinking Disruptive Discovery *is a bad thing, think again and start reading immediately. Geoff breaks these words down in a conversational flow that demonstrates the power of emotional connections with the people that we support. You might be a new manager, a team leader, or a high-level executive. Perhaps you are in the business of helping customers, as either a sales professional in training or a seasoned veteran. Or maybe you are a valued adviser for family and friends in everyday life. This book is a great resource in all of these areas and will enable you to make an impact.*

—Steve Willis, President, AdvantaClean

This book challenges the foundation of how we approach helping people achieve their personal and professional development. But Geoff Snavely pulls it off through a funny, easily readable, and compelling experience. Disruptive Discovery *is an invitation to growth that so many people need.*

—Michael Peluso, CEO True Living, Entrepreneur, Coach, and Speaker

DISRUPTIVE
DISCOVERY

Uncovering the Stuff
That REALLY Matters

BY GEOFF SNAVELY

**DISRUPTIVE
PRESS**

Copyright ©2021 by Geoff Snavely

All rights reserved. No part of this book may be used or reproduced in any manner whatsoever without written permission except in the case of brief quotations embodied in critical articles or reviews.

Published by Disruptive Press

Paperback ISBN: 978-1-7379571-0-2
ebook ISBN: 978-1-7379571-1-9

Printed in the United States of America
10 9 8 7 6 5 4 3 2 1

Produced by GMK Writing and Editing, Inc.
Copyedited and Proofread by Randy Ladenheim-Gil
Text design and composition by Libby Kingsbury
Cover design by Libby Kingsbury
Index by Joan Shapiro
Printed by IngramSpark

iPod, iPad, Mac, and related Apple products are registered trademarks (R) of Apple, Inc.

Visit Geoff Snavely at disruptivediscovery.com
You can also contact Geoff directly by emailing him at: geoff@disruptivediscovery.com

Dedicated to Ella, Alex, and Katharene.
Thank you for helping me discover life in the most miraculously
disruptive way. I love you more than words could ever express, so I
won't even try because any attempt would be found wanting. Just know
that I will do everything within my power to prove it every
day by giving you the best of my heart and mind.

DON'T HOPE FOR BETTER. JUST BE BETTER.

—MARK MANSON

CONTENTS

AN OVERSHARING-FILLED INTRODUCTION

This will be brief, I promise. But I guess "brief" is a relative term, so maybe I should try again.

I will get to my point as quickly as possible, I promise. That's more like it.

I'm going to take a wild guess that there are a few questions you might be asking yourself right now:

Who is this guy?

Why did he write a book?

Hey, wait! Why am I reading his book?

These are great questions. I can't promise to have great answers to them, but I can try. Here goes...

In my personal life, I'm a pretty average middle-aged guy. I married an amazing woman who showed me that my life could have more meaning than I ever imagined. I have two Daughters who both stole my heart the instant I looked into their eyes. It wasn't even a fair fight. I never had a chance.

From a professional standpoint, I am part owner of a commercial floor care company. Yes, that's right, I clean carpet for a living, but let me be very clear about something...I PROUDLY clean carpet for a living and am incredibly grateful for my career path. I'm passionate about taking care of our customers and employees. I can only hope for many more years of continuing to grow these relationships that mean so much to me.

I love my family, I love my friends, and I love my company. I consider myself fortunate in so many ways. Life is good. There simply aren't many reasons for me to complain. Sure, on some days I fall into the trap of an unreasonable, entitled feeling in which I think life sucks and the planet is focused solely on making me miserable. But I usually find perspective, get over myself, and realize, once again, that life is good. I try to practice gratitude as much as possible but have learned it can be elusive, like an engine that needs constant tune-ups.

I don't really spend time on social media. Not saying that's a good thing or a bad thing. It just isn't a priority for me. In fact, I have never been on Facebook, Instagram, Snapchat, or TikTok*. I do have a Twitter "handle" from a long time ago, but I can't give a good explanation for having it, other than incorrectly thinking it could somehow help from a business standpoint. My only significant social media activity is through LinkedIn. This is only important to mention because I obviously don't have a following of people waiting to hear my thoughts, other than my family, friends, and professional contacts. And I'm pretty sure they're either listening under protest or just plain being nice. But, at a minimum, they hear what's on my mind. At least, I think they do. Maybe they're zoning out and only pretending to listen. *You* hear me right? Now that I hear *myself*, it would be tough to blame them.

Over the years, I developed some very strange sleeping patterns. I'm not talking about insomnia or recapturing the glory days of college and sleeping until early afternoon. No, these were just weird sleeping behaviors that seemed to happen for no real reason, lasted for a little while, and changed into different, stranger patterns. It all started with simply waking up ridiculously early. I would be wide-eyed and full of energy. Instead of fighting it and trying to force myself back to sleep or staring

---

*Funny how things change. The claims I made about my social media ineptness were absolutely true at the time those words were typed. Since that time, I now eat a steady diet of those words every day. As you read this footnote, I have bloomed into a social media icon. Is there an emoji for "I clearly didn't mean that"? If so, pretend to insert one here because I don't know how to type them...and they creep me out. I might not be the sharpest bulb (get it?) but I'm no dummy either. It didn't take long in the publishing process to figure out that book promotion without social media is more like book demotion. So, I quickly sold my soul. It wasn't difficult. I put a listing on Facebook Marketplace. The devil contacted me right away.

at the ceiling for a few worthless hours, I embraced being awake. I would grab my running shoes and go for a jaunt around our very dark and quiet neighborhood. Maybe I'd go to the gym or find some other activity to pass the time until I could start the daily routine at a somewhat more normal time without waking my family. I became a creepy night crawler.

That lasted for a little while, and then things got weirder. I started sleeping twice each night. Yeah, like I said, it was weird. I would conk out without any trouble every night and naturally wake up at around midnight. Again, I realized trying to brawl with whatever was happening in my body and brain was an exercise in futility. Figured it was simply better to go with the flow. I would get out of bed, go down into the basement, and find some activity to pass the time. Perhaps it was knocking out a few emails or watching one of my favorite binge-worthy series (more on my TV watching in a minute). I would predictably get tired about an hour later, crawl back into bed, and easily fall asleep again until it was time to start the regular morning routine. But I felt great. No fatigue or health issues. Just a bizarre way to get through the night.

Lately, I've finally settled into a less strange, but still incredibly annoying sleep pattern. Benjamin Franklin famously said, "Early to bed and early to rise, makes a man healthy, wealthy, and wise." Well, Ben lived until the age of eighty-four, made a few bucks, and obviously knew a thing or two because we're still quoting him several hundred years later. So, perhaps there is some merit to the whole early-to-bed, early-to-rise thing. But I would give just about anything to sleep past sunrise one day. And my Daughters think I'm superlame for falling asleep most nights while they're still doing their homework, talking with their friends, or anything other than social media because that's not their thing. Sorry, I just choked a little, trying to swallow a laugh.

Anyway, I find myself bright-eyed and bushy-tailed sometime between four and five a.m. every morning. Unfortunately, it's the same thing even if I've had a few too many drinks the previous night, though minus some brightness and bushiness. My routine is fairly consistent. I jump out of bed, pour a giant bowl of cereal—the sugary, kids' type, containing Puffs, Pops, or Pebbles, please—hustle down the steps into my quiet, dark basement dungeon, and get going on a variety of activities while everyone else is happily sawing logs. Usually, it's a combination of work-related bustle and nonproductive, yet very satisfying, TV watching. I often use this time for a morning run or workout as well.

Recently, I decided all of these precious moments could be used for something more substantial. The middle of the night emails could be sent a few hours later, so recipients would no longer start their responses with, "Why are you sending me emails at 4:14 a.m.?" And my morning run or workout could wait until, I don't know, there are actually other human beings outside. I could watch *Mad Men* or *Grey's Anatomy* at night. Yes, I said *Grey's Anatomy*. Cut me some slack, OK? It's a guilty pleasure, and I compare notes about plot lines with my teenage Daughters as a bonding experience. While I'm confessing embarrassing secrets, I'll also go ahead and admit to being a die-hard Neil Diamond fan too. Want more? OK. I dig me some Journey and will own up to knowing the lyrics of a shameful number of Air Supply songs. Do you know what's wrong with a love ballad? Not a damn thing! Hey, I watched *Sopranos* and *Breaking Bad* too. And Guns N' Roses rules! Don't even get me started on my love for '80s hair bands. Sorry for that minirant, but my TV and music habits are an exposed nerve and I'm a tad bit defensive in case you haven't noticed.

Back to my crazy early morning routine. How could I use this time for a more meaningful purpose? I'm glad you asked. Somewhere along my journey in life, I realized that I actually might have something to say. Something that could perhaps make a positive difference. Years of observing people, listening to their problems, making lots of my own mistakes, learning from them, and benefiting from nuggets passed along by several incredible mentors has provided me with, I dare say, wisdom. If that word is too ambitious, I apologize. Let's just say I feel as if I have some insights that can possibly do some good for people in their lives, both personally and professionally. And I sincerely believe that if people have something compelling to say, something potentially impactful, they should say it. And that is precisely what I decided to do.

This book is my attempt to share what's on my mind in an attempt to help others interested in getting to a better place. I have a strong desire to impart the thoughts and ideas in which I feel impassioned. Will they help you? I hope so. Let's find out…

PART ONE

SETTING THE STAGE

1

WHY DISRUPTIVE DISCOVERY?

want to make sure we get off on the right foot, so I have a confession to make…

I'm NOT a writer. How's that for irony?

Once again, it should be pointed out that I proudly and passionately clean floors for a living. This toe-in-the-water attempt at authorship is a humbling, and possibly nutty, new frontier.

With that out of the way, if it's OK with you, I will begin with some deep thoughts. Is there a better way to start a book and put readers to sleep in no time flat than an amateur philosopher pontificating on their überdramatic ramblings? I don't think so.

In the book *Start with Why*, Simon Sinek challenges people and companies to find their purpose. For me, that purpose—*my* WHY—is to make a positive difference in the lives of other people, both personally and professionally, so they feel motivated to become the best possible versions of themselves.

See, I already hear the snoozing. That was a labyrinthine way of saying that, at my core, I want to help people. I do. It's just that the manner in which I try to achieve that purpose isn't what you might call traditional.

I am 100 percent in support of giving time and money to charities and other philanthropic endeavors. That's not what this book is about. There are many methods and means to lend a hand. And this is the avenue I have bear-hugged as my way of offering support and aid to people, if they so desire. I guess you could say this is my attempt at doing what I can to help make the world a better place.

As predicted, I have a feeling this strikes you as an average guy being dramatic and heavy. But I am genuinely talking from the heart. That must count for something. Mustn't it?

Now, let's *really* have some fun and talk about math. I mean, everyone loves math, right? But don't worry. I won't be getting into algebra, or even long division. Let's start with an equation I'm assuming was the first-ever problem to be solved in the history of math. Are you ready?

$$1 + 1 = ?$$

Come on, you got this. Yes, the obvious answer we all learned at a very young age is 2, but I'm sure you've already realized this was a setup. A way for me to make a brilliant point challenging one of the most basic truths in life. An important message that will shift paradigms, raise the bar, and inflame outside-the-box thinking. Oh, by the way, I should come clean with something about myself before proceeding much further. I'm a sarcasm buff and I use it excessively as a crutch.

Those overused clichés are a little too dramatic for this conversation. But sometimes clichés exist for a reason. In many cases, they became clichés in the first place due to being on target and earning the right. The cliché I want to use to begin this conversation about discovery is also the answer to our math equation.

$$1 + 1 = 3$$

This is clearly not the correct answer in kindergarten or when balancing your checkbook. However, for our purposes, understanding such a core concept is foundational to the time we'll spend together. Sometimes adding things together equals something greater than the sum of their parts. It's like sleight of hand or witchcraft. But no hocus-pocus here. This mathbuster is the quintessence of Disruptive Discovery.

Two words. Each with their own unique meaning and definitions. On their own, each word has value and significance. But when put together, their potency increases exponentially. Combining those two words—disruptive and discovery—makes something special happen. It gives energy and meaning to the cliché.

Disruptive + Discovery = Game Changer

The ideology of Disruptive Discovery is one of the ways in which I can bring my WHY to life. You see, I'm not good at much of anything. Really, I'm not. But this is a skill I have cultivated over the years. It has evolved through experiences, observations, and applications of learning. I am fascinated with people and the things they do every day. If I ever build a time machine, I'll probably go back just a few decades and study anthropology.

Yes, I realize that constructing a time machine would be somewhat unprecedented and, if given the chance, you would probably do something much more thrilling with the ability to time travel. But this is my fantasy and my boringness. Invent your own time machine!

Anyway, anthropology would give a basis for understanding why people do what they do. Unfortunately, I haven't figured out how to assemble one of those handy contraptions, and I'm far too old and lazy to get my degree in anthropology at this stage. So, I will just keep on keepin' on, coming up with other means of amassing theories about people and their behavior.

Much of that experimentation is done through routinely putting ideas into practice. Whether they be my own or from another origin, I am constantly looking for opportunities to apply and test different notions. In some cases, conjecture about a viewpoint or premise in its infancy stage is disproved and either tweaked or discarded. The B-side to those records are the times when a suspicion is confirmed and further refined. Either way, these thoughts, theories, ideas, or whatever else I am trying to reconcile are continually in a state of flux, evolving or devolving.

Fortunately, a long time ago, I started keeping stashes of notes to myself in an effort to capture all these works in progress. Many have been recorded and kept in scatterings of electronic documents. Others have simply been saved in a mental vault, so to speak. It seems like my favorites tend to fall in the latter category, committed to memory and always readily accessible. I would say this practice began sometime in my early twenties, right after realizing that my interest in human behavior was more than a mild curiosity.

Somewhere in the midst of these nomadic follies, the fog lifted and I had a light-bulb-over-the-head moment. As I was trying to understand the reason for my fascination with human behavior, a compelling realization emerged for me.

My steadfast preoccupation in unraveling why people do what they do was missing a key ingredient. It was lacking an endgame. What was I doing with those learnings and observations? I challenged myself on whether these efforts were purely to satisfy my own curiosity or to provide some form of entertainment. As it turned out, I wasn't guilty of such a depthless whyfor. Not at all. Oppositely, this awakening manifested into something much more worthwhile because I realized how the potential of understanding human behavior could be truly fulfilled.

Enlightenment.

Wait! Before you slam the book shut and throw it across the room, I am not talking about spiritual enlightenment or anything in that vicinity. I am referring to gaining insights about ourselves. Stay with me...

Understanding why people do what they do = Good to know.

People understanding *themselves* and why *they do what they do* = Welcome to the new world.

And then it hit me. Maybe all my scribblings and borderline lucid thoughts might be useful after all. I decided the channel in which I was best equipped to help people was through shedding the sort of light that can lead to self-awareness. With that recognition, individuals can gain an invaluable understanding of why they do what they do. Or, equally important, why they DON'T do what they WANT to do.

I had no idea this newfound purpose would eventually become a book, but, hey, stranger things have happened. At least, I hope stranger things have happened. Otherwise, I'd better pull the chute. In fairness, you are the only suitable judge regarding the strangeness of this writing project. I should circle back with you for a verdict in a few hundred pages, right?

What you're reading is my attempt to synthesize everything that has been sticking in my skull like barnacles. These contemplative crustaceans have formed by combining takeaways from a vast array of different sources and countless observations with an inordinate amount of common sense as a double-check measure. I had to do a pressure washing and get them out of there! So, this is a download of those learnings I've managed to accumulate through my personal and professional wanderings. All of which I am eternally grateful for, by the way.

At the end of the day, if passing along the stuff on my mind could somehow help others get themselves to a better place, that would be pretty amazing. I sincerely hope this book serves as a resource for anyone attempting to make that happen.

Before we unleash the force that erupts when putting "disruptive" and "discovery" together, it would be advisable to establish some definitions for each. The best place to start is "discovery."

2

WHAT'S MY DEAL WITH DISCOVERY ANYWAY?

For as long as I can remember, I have enjoyed asking questions. No, that's a tremendous understatement. I am *zealous* about asking questions. Call me an avid asker or some other name and I will say, "Abso-freaking-lutely!" If my colleagues, friends, or family members were eavesdropping, they would agree, and perhaps even say this is a big part of my identity. We could also expect a rolling of the eyes in there somewhere. To some people, Geoff is the "annoying question guy."

Let me give you an example. Every Thanksgiving, and I do mean EVERY Thanksgiving, I torture my family—and anyone else unlucky enough to be in the wrong place at the wrong time—with a question to which I have never heard a good answer.

Why was pumpkin pie invented?

Don't get me wrong, I love pumpkin pie. I am gaga over pumpkin pie, and no Thanksgiving is complete for me without eating a few too many slices. Its existence has made me a happier person, but I don't understand how this delicious miracle ever found its way into an oven and onto our Thanksgiving dinner table. Confused? Hang in there. This is going somewhere.

Have you ever eaten pumpkin? No, not pumpkin bread or pumpkin seeds. And a pumpkin spice latte doesn't count either. (That's just a flavor made from things we probably would rather remain top-secret intellectual property.) I'm talking about pumpkin. A big ol' serving of pumpkin.

That's what I thought. It's not something you eat as a stand-alone food. Not baked, grilled, sautéed, deep fried, or mashed. So, if we don't eat pumpkin on its own, who in tarnation decided that it would make a great pie? I'm imagining some really bored Pilgrims four hundred years ago coming across a pumpkin in a field and saying to themselves, "You know what? I would never take a bite out of that crazy orange thing laying in the dirt, but I'll bet it would make a killer pie!"

Should I keep going? OK. Name one other pie whose featured ingredient you wouldn't eat on its own. Go ahead. See? Yet somehow, pumpkin pie has a prominent place in the Pie Hall of Fame.

It should be noted that rhubarb and lime are the most common rebuttals to my hypothesis. I am embarrassed to say that I have performed "research" on those two, and they are consumed on their own quite regularly. All you tequila drinkers know exactly what I'm talking about (concerning limes, not rhubarb, but after a few shots of tequila I guess anything is possible.)

Like I said. Annoying. But I honestly don't believe it's a frivolous question. I genuinely want to know the answer. This is just one example of perhaps a gabillion—I'm planning to start a petition to make it a certified number—and curiosity is constantly flowing through my brain. For me, inquisitiveness takes the form of asking incessant questions and, as you can imagine, receives a mixed bag of results.

A Love Triangle: Questions, Me, and Discovery

If I'm being honest, I've often found myself exhausted because of this inescapable need to understand most of what I encounter. It's either a gift or a curse, depending on your perspective. In both personal and professional settings, I have viewed this personality trait as either positive or negative, depending on the situation. If the person I'm talking to seemed to enjoy the conversation and found value in exploring my questions with me, I felt a boost of confidence and pride in the ability to assist someone in broadening their horizons. On the flip side, if these thinking exercises and searches for answers frustrated the other person, or even a group of people, to the point that they either found an excuse to run away or simply stared at me with glazed eyes, I spent some time evaluating this relationship-damaging character flaw and asked myself what I could do to prevent launching lead-filled balloons in the future.

After countless such situations and an overwhelming amount of soul-searching, I learned something about myself. I became aware of the reason asking questions is so important to me. And this epiphany has absolutely nothing to do with being annoying, a way to pass time, or some bizarre curiosity. Nope. I simply embrace the power of discovery. And this self-realization has proven to be very powerful.

Sounds like some serious gibberish I'm feeding myself to justify socially unacceptable behavior, huh? Not so fast.

We can take a look at how the dictionary defines discovery. One definition is "to make known or visible." Another is "to obtain sight for the first time." And they confirm a working definition that is crystal clear in my mind:

uncovering something new

That's how I have grown to view discovery and the doors it can open, especially in the mind. This interpretation captures the spirit of those dictionary definitions. The challenge is that discovery has limitations unless it leads us to true insights. In other words, uncovering something new is a fine accomplishment, but if it doesn't make an impact, so what? If a discovery doesn't ultimately lead to an enhanced outcome, who cares? Ah, but we *should* care.

Let Me Count the Ways

Discovery can open our eyes to fresh possibilities and prospects through several distinct routes. On the most basic level, discovery expands awareness. It represents a pathway for being exposed or introduced to something for the first time. Those eye-opening encounters could be anything from finding a penny in the parking lot, to reading a thought-provoking passage in an article, to feeling that life-changing love for your child. We're talking about ideas, activities, and an unlimited number of other examples including, between, and outside those extremes. It's through discovery in this context that we are able to develop new skills, improve existing capabilities, or advance ourselves in areas that can make us better.

Take note that discoveries can be material or abstract in nature. I must emphasize the importance of mindset in discovery. It would be such a rarity to discover something new with a closed mind. Please never, ever, ever, ever, ever lose sight of this verity. Yes, this even includes the penny example; think about it. Therefore, we will assume an open mind is firmly in place from this point forward, until you're done with me. It's a prerequisite. Deal?

Next, discovery can be a strong ally in finding solutions to problems. Maybe "challenge" or "opportunity" is the preferred terminology these days, but you get the point. Basically, I'm talking about being faced with something that just ain't right and needs fixin'. Once again, this applies to the wide range of problems we encounter on a daily basis. Those dilemmas will differ in severity and complexity. There are so many different issues, predicaments, obstacles, and pickles, it would be almost impossible to list all categories. Some involve other people and some don't. Some are technical and others are ethical. The possibilities are almost limitless. But all problems have something in common. All of them.

They need solutions to be resolved.

How do we determine the right solution? You guessed it. Discovery. The idea is to identify the option that will best address the unique needs of the specific problem, challenge, opportunity, or whatever you want to call it.

Finally, discovery plays an important role in building and maintaining relationships. This is true in any relationship, regardless of who it involves, when it started, how it came about, or where it takes place. Discovery is an efficacious tool for gaining an understanding of other people and their values, interests, fears, goals, and perspectives on a wide range of topics. In the process of discovery, you can learn concurrently whether you share things in common, while also bring into the open areas in which you see the world differently.

Relationship building doesn't only take place with other individuals. It occurs in groups, communities, organizations, companies, and other entities. Discovering the internal dynamics of these parties and the manner in which they operate is principal in growing connections or is a factor in determining lack of fit.

Are there other areas in which discovery has a place? I suppose. But I would argue that I've covered the overwhelming majority. And if you suggested another scenario, my guess is that it could be associated within one of these buckets.

So, we have established the significant importance of discovery in our everyday lives. If used effectively, it can help us get to a better place in a variety of ways. But that doesn't just happen magically. And discovery certainly reaches different levels of success and results from person to person, situation to situation. It requires skill, practice, focus, and dedication to consistently realize the best outcomes. We will talk in detail about how to achieve excellence with discovery in later chapters.

That's my deal with discovery. How'd I do with justifying my obsession?

Before we start outlining how to put discovery into action, though, we need to explore one more concept, and it's a big one.

Ice cream is awesome. That gift of frozen bliss is supernatural in my book. I mean, who can resist ice cream? And there's no such thing as a bad ice cream either. It's physically impossible. Granted, some flavors are better than others, but they're all good. Never met a spoonful I didn't like.

For just a moment, let's imagine that ice cream only came in one flavor. As tragic as this hypothetical nightmare sounds, ice cream would still be great. I mean, it's ice cream. But the mystique of ice cream is somewhat linked to the boundless optionality of flavors. That means having lots of them! Whatever your mood, you can find a flavor to match it perfectly.

If you're wondering why I'm off on an ice cream tangent, I hear you. There's a point to this divergence. The connector is that discovery is similar to ice cream in this regard: There is more than a single type of discovery, just as ice cream isn't limited to only one flavor. Each has its place and leads to unique experiences. With discovery, though, we aren't talking about an unlimited number of different flavors. From where I stand, there are only two.

And we're off...

3

STARTING ON THE SURFACE

Now that we have established a working definition of discovery, identified the areas in which it functions, and stated that there are two different types, you might be thinking, "OK, dude. Are you going to give me more details, or was this just a ploy for you to spread propaganda about kid's cereal, pie, and ice cream?" That's a legitimate question, and I'll get directly to the point, for once. In my mind, based on no shortage of practice and experiences, there are two primary types of discovery:

- Surface
- Disruptive

These two forms have specialized implications. One is not better or worse than the other. This isn't about good or bad. Judgment has no place in this conversation because both are valuable in the multitude of ways we have discussed the potential for discovery to make a difference and influence outcomes. Both Surface Discovery and Disruptive Discovery have important roles to play. They just don't take shape in the same way.

Scratching the...

Surface Discovery is mostly self-explanatory, but I'll elaborate a little bit. When something sits on the surface, it lacks depth. I realize that's a statement of obviousness. However, something alleged to be obvious doesn't necessarily warrant a sentence of insignificance. In many cases, the opposite is true. In those instances, the obvious needs to be stated so its importance is clear and appropriately emphasized. This is one of those situations.

Discovery on a surface level helps us gain basic knowledge and understanding. This type of information is extremely useful in the early stages of expanding awareness, problem-solving, and relationship building. The relevance of the information learned carries forward into future stages of those processes. These learnings help to establish connections with other information gathered and can serve as a catalyst for generating more. As the level of knowledge and understanding grows, the foundation enlarges and strengthens. From that point, opportunities can present themselves to potentially pursue different possibilities for building on those foundations.

Actually, it's the opposite, or maybe the foundation reference is counterintuitive. Instead of building higher, as you would on most foundations, the goal is to dig deeper.

It's important to mention that a range of depth does, in fact, exist at this surface level. At one extreme, the information shared can be overly basic, encroaching on the trivial. But as you move along the spectrum that exists in this type of discovery, more meaningful and valuable knowledge can be gained. These nuggets of information might play at a relatively shallow level simply because they aren't necessarily compelling or immediately actionable. But that shouldn't diminish or minimalize their significance in the big picture of a comprehensive discovery process. Surface Discovery is needed for transitioning into a deeper level of understanding, which will be outlined in Chapter 10. In the meantime, just know that important information about individuals, groups, companies, or problems can be obtained at this level of discovery.

The Work-Life Balance of Discovery

That leads us to a very interesting point in our discussion. I have mentioned friends, family, colleagues, groups, and companies. You might be wondering about personal versus professional scenarios in the context of discovery. Maybe you're wondering, "Is the discovery process different between my personal and professional lives?" That's a fantastic question. And I'll give you a fantastic answer.

Yes…and no.

How's that for wishy-washy? I really put myself out there with that one. But the truth is the truth and I have a commitment to it.

We should take a minute to put my response of duality to the test. This can be done by overlaying it with the relationships people form with one another. On one hand, the concept of discovery and its worth in relationship building holds water on both the personal and the professional level. In general, discovery looks more similar than different when it's taking place with friends or family versus coworkers, customers, your boss, or other professional colleagues. At its core, the process of uncovering something new in relationships involves asking questions, listening to the answers, understanding what was specifically said or inferred, being aware of what was *not* specifically said or inferred, and knowing what to do with the knowledge gained.

Plus, there is an undeniable reality that overlap and gray areas exist with people in our professional lives. Friendships and other connections can obviously evolve from relationships that start in the workplace.

However, on the other hand, the specific dynamics of personal versus professional relationships are apples and oranges. Those ties usually exist for drastically distinct and diverse purposes. I would be willing to bet that most people could point to some professional relationships that are simply not optional. Efforts to establish a strong working relationship might be required for certain job responsibilities and goals. We also know that many of these links are transactional in nature. And, in more unfavorable circumstances, they could represent a necessary evil or have that sinking condition-of-employment feeling. As a result, the types of questions, how they are asked, and what is done with the answers might look very different in those environments.

More importantly, the chosen manner in which you build trust in personal relationships might not closely resemble your approach in a professional domain. Yet, establishing trust is absolutely critical in the discovery process, especially with Disruptive Discovery. Get used to seeing that word, because a trust tidal wave has been spotted offshore. But, for now, I'll just give a spoiler alert…without trust, there is no need to talk about Disruptive Discovery. Nothing would be learned beyond what's on the surface level. Yes, this would save you some time because it wouldn't be necessary to read much further. But aren't we having fun?

The thinking regarding comparing personal and professional lives holds true with the other areas in which discovery plays a role. Whether you're trying to solve a problem or becoming aware of something for the first time, there are similarities and differences with these activities in those distinct universes. And, once again, the process looks more similar than different. It really becomes a question of purpose and context. In other words, your attachment to a dilemma being solved at work will have a particular resonance compared to resolving a problem at home, even if you go about determining the cause using the same methodology. Or a key takeaway from a seminar at a professional conference will probably be applied in a way dissimilar to one of those proverbial "aha!" moments from your most recent self-help book or podcast, even with the same critical thinking technique being tapped.

Circling back to trust, there is no denying its leverage in problem-solving and expanding awareness. And the presence of personalities, emotions, risks, and other variables are very much in the fold with those personal and professional scenarios.

See what I mean? Simultaneously demonstrating contrasts and harmonies. This is one of those pesky paradoxes.

Maybe a few more examples of information shared during Surface Discovery in different situations will offer a little more clarity. Let's say you're at a party and are introduced to someone for the first time. You might engage in a nice conversation with this person covering many of the traditional small talk topics. There could be pleasantries shared about hometowns, what you do for a living, and your family situations (marriage, kids, pet guinea pigs, and in-laws living in the basement). Some lively dialogue could be sparked about favorite sports teams, bands, or hobbies. Recent trips or upcoming travel? Where else have you lived? How about a favorite movie or book? And, of course, the Old Faithful of chit-chat topics…how 'bout this weather we're having?

Do you notice anything there strictly for personal settings? Nope. If this were a business event, no professional lines would be crossed discussing any of those topics. However, the party conversation could easily transition into areas you might want to avoid in the office. Heck, you might want to avoid certain conversations completely in all situations. But certainly there are some socially acceptable topics that, if launched by someone while hanging around the watercooler at work, might have you considering employing the ruse of suddenly remembering a meeting that started five minutes ago. I think we've learned the no-fly zone of topics to avoid in professional settings: age, sex, religion, and politics, to name a few. Again, you might want to stay away from these potential land mines in your personal life in new or long-standing relationships, but they carry a much higher risk, with zero reward, in your professional life.

Conversely, I can't imagine many new acquaintances met at the birthday party of your five-year-old daughter's bestie want to hear about your current project timeline, a competitive analysis of your company's latest product launch, or the PowerPoint slides you're presenting to your boss on Monday morning. They don't give a crap, even if they feign giving a crap, and you shouldn't assume they have a crap to give.

With problem-solving, the specific challenges you're trying to resolve at home are most likely very different from the ones you're facing at work, but the methods of uncovering solutions themselves would be homogenous. Examples of discovery applications in your professional life could be trying to help a customer with a frustration they're facing or collaborating with a coworker on the agenda for an upcoming department meeting in which you need to discuss some controversial topics. Or maybe you and your office buddy are struggling to decide where to grab lunch that day. However, in your personal life, you might be engaged in different types of "collaborations." Yes, I realize I just used quotation marks. That's because I am fully aware that collaborating with your son on how to improve time management habits or make better decisions about social media activity might sound more like, well, arguing (and that's probably a generous description).

There are probably an infinite number of challenges faced in your personal life that would never happen in the workplace. And then there'd be another list of predicaments that should never happen in the workplace, but that's another story. However, overlap or common themes might exist at the root of any problem, regardless of their settings. Better time management, improved decision-making, fixing broken processes, efficient planning, and creating budgets are just a few examples of development opportunities that exist in both personal and professional realms, with different participants and backdrops involved.

This yin and yang concept also applies to experiences that expand our awareness. These exposure opportunities more than likely target specific audiences and designed payoffs. But there is minuscule doubt that many of the takeaways arising from your professional learning environments have applications on a personal level, and vice versa.

As you can see, there is an expansive collection of examples with commonality in both worlds. But there's also an extensive number of situations that simply wouldn't be interchangeable in your personal or professional lives. Does discovery look the same professionally as it does personally? No…yes…it depends.

Celebrating the Differences of Both Discovery Types

Remember, we've mostly been talking about Surface Discovery up until this moment. As I mentioned earlier, blurred lines are more likely at this stage. But when we delve into Disruptive Discovery, you'll realize the two domains are much more diverse. Put another way, the deeper we go in the process, the more discernable the distinction will become, and the presence of any overlap will be greatly reduced, if not eliminated completely.

I wanted to make one final point about Surface Discovery. This version of discovery typifies the comfort zone for most people. It's the default probing system we instinctively favor when conducting ourselves. And the overwhelming majority of activities in the areas explored so far center around what is uncovered at a surface level. As we have astutely acknowledged, there's a range of depth at work, but, make no mistake, most personal and professional learnings, problems, and relationships never get into the deep end of the pool. And that's totally fine. This commentary about Surface Discovery is in no way meant to give a pessimistic outlook.

After all, we're still playing out our ice cream analogy. If someone handed me a bowl of vanilla, you would hear no complaints from this guy. Vanilla ice cream is a classic for good reason, even if French vanilla is my preferred offshoot.

I'm simply saying that the possibility exists for more meaningful relationships. And better solutions. And impactfully elevated awareness. That's beginning to sound like chocolate ice cream with cookie dough chunks, brownie batter, miniature peanut butter cups, toffee pieces, and a gooey fudge swirl. That flavor would be called Disruptive Discovery, and I could really go for a triple dip right about now.

As we start to shift gears, step on the gas, and head in that direction, I can't emphasize enough that what you'll see and hear once we arrive at our destination will be a new experience. The scenery will look unfamiliar and the locals speak an exotic dialect. That language is the other type of discovery, and it's the predominant emphasis of this book. We're getting there. You have my word.

To make the transition, we desperately need to find a sorting gadget or thingamabob, whichever is most readily available. This little-known machine separates the "nice to know" from the "we can do something with *that*." In that vein, and keeping in the context of Disruptive Discovery, we must be vigilant about seeking knowledge that can make a difference.

The stuff that really matters.

But how do we know what meets that standard? What information can lead us to positive change? To shed some light on these questions, we need to challenge the paradigm of what it means to be…

All together now…

Disruptive.

4

BUT ISN'T BEING DISRUPTIVE A BAD THING?

When we were kids, being disruptive was far removed from something that would garner the praise of parents, teachers, or authority figures. In fact, I can remember many situations in which disruptive behavior in school led to my classmates getting sent into exile in the principal's office or imprisoned in dreaded detention. Yes, you heard correctly. My classmates. Not me. Never. Man, I wish. Those detention slips are engraved in my adolescent memory. At my school they were either yellow (minor) or pink (major) and had a chemical smell I'll never forget. It was the smell of shame and is forever etched.

Grown-ups also exhibit disruptive behavior, unfortunately. A colleague arriving late for a meeting or a coworker answering their phone in the middle of a group discussion makes it difficult for everyone else to stay focused on the task at hand. What about the "adult" at a holiday party who maybe knocks back a few too many eggnogs and stumbles around the room, making offensive and inappropriate comments to other guests?

There are other examples of disruptive events that are problematic. Natural disasters are poster children for disruption on many devastating levels. Power outages, traffic accidents, stock market crashes, and a dropped Wi-Fi connection are also havoc-wreaking disruptions.

But let's flip this conversation upside down and consider the benefits that can result from being disruptive. I think we should take a contrarian—mental note for what's to come later—point of view and consider the awesomeness of being disruptive.

What Did He Just Say?

When an event or activity is disruptive, it stimulates change. We should ruminate over that word for a spell.

CHANGE

In the above examples, the type of change precipitated from those disruptions run the gamut from mildly inconvenient to calamitous. However, a turn of events is also capable of the exact opposite effect. Those changes can lead to positive outcomes.

We also know that change is typically not instigated willy-nilly. In most cases, something weighty must happen for change to take place. So, when talking about disruptive events or activities, it could be implied that they carry significance, importance, or consequence.

Disruption challenges the status quo. That can lead to new thinking or adjustments in existing plans. Disruptions often encourage individuals to look at situations or people, including themselves, through a different lens, try out diverse ways of thinking, or engage in new conversations.

There are so many instances of disruptive events that have taken place throughout history. Technology innovations such as the Internet or smartphones certainly have created an overwhelming magnitude of change in our lives. The Amazon delivery truck showing up at my doorstep every day probably qualifies. Oh, and let's not forget about fire, the wheel, and electricity. Those discoveries happened quite a few years ago but have certainly been disruptive, to say the least. If you believe referring to the wheel as a discovery as opposed to an invention is technically incorrect, I disagree. And I would welcome the opportunity to debate my rationale. Pick a pub and I'll see you there.

My point is that events and other activities we consider disruptive are not categorically negative. In fact, as exhibited in a few examples previously mentioned, the opposite of negative came to pass and society benefited staggeringly. Does change result from disruptions? No question. But change isn't necessarily a bad thing.

Quick sidebar…

Upon making the decision to get serious about becoming a writer—and I'm making that self-proclamation very loosely—I had a conversation with myself. Like most of the banter taking place in my head, it quickly deteriorated into a full-blown argument. This particular disagreement emanated from the level of profanity I would incorporate in my writing style. If I wanted to achieve a truly conversational tone, I figured lots of swearing and four-letter words should be used because, well, people cuss a lot when chewing the fat. That's how we talk to one another when we let our hair down. If you don't share that vice with the rest of us heathens, my apologies for being so presumptuous. Just know that I tried to exercise sensitivity about not wanting to offend anyone or come across as barbaric. After lots of yelling, name-calling, and throwing things at myself, I decided to compromise…with myself. The middle ground was an allowance of four relatively harmless offenses of profane language.

I'm sure four sounds like an arbitrary number to you. What I would give for such a throwaway explanation. Let's just say I have a minor—depending on who you ask—case of OCD. In the depths of my personal grab bag of symptoms for this so-much-fun condition is a real beaut. I get to thoroughly enjoy the pleasure of an avoidance to the number three whenever possible. And sixes are unspeakable. Don't ask. Just roll with it.

And so it goes. Because two bad words weren't enough, and restricting vulgarity to only a sole transaction was completely off the table, I settled on four. On a scale from one to ten, with ten being a bar-of-soap-sucking offense, the specific word I selected would score a three…

Chills…twitch…shiver…sweat…

Upon further review, I'll rate it as a four, just to be safe. You'll see these instances of mild obscenities scattered throughout the coming pages. It can be like a literary Easter egg hunt.

Ready, set, end of sidebar…

How many times have you heard someone say, "People don't like change"? This comment is made constantly, with the uttermost confidence and certainty. It sometimes feels like they're saying the sky is blue, water is wet, or it sucks getting old (it does!). But guess what pops into my puritanical brain when I hear someone state this widely accepted fact of life. Yup, right on cue.

Bullshit.

Frequent utterances of projected disdain for change is an example of an illusory truth effect we encounter and to which we unknowingly capitulate on a regular basis. Ever heard of an illusory truth effect? That was a silly question. Of course you've heard of it. I'll further explain, just in case, because I find this tendency fascinating. An illusory truth effect is basically something that takes place when people accept false information after hearing it often enough. With that in mind, there's another factor supporting why people repeat this statement about not liking change and wave the flag of the misconception over and over. Confirmation bias, yet another tendency, shares culpability. This sweet talker comes out to play when we're looking for information that supports our preexisting beliefs.

It's not that people don't like change. They're just scared of losing anything important to them. Or, at least, anything they *think* is important to them. But in so many cases, change actually helps people improve their situations, potentially even their lives. In those situations, instead of losing old, important possessions, they actually gain new, more important possessions.

No, what people don't usually like about the change process has nothing to do with the change itself. It has more to do with how change is handled. Lack of communication, no buy-in, and not being involved are ordeals that contribute to the myth. Those ills can lead to people resisting changes that, in reality, represent their best interests. Departures from "as is" can so often do a lot of good. Ultimately, the individuals involved might like the change but resent the manner in which it went down.

We get to enjoy some of the most incredible parts of our lives today, both personally and professionally, because change happened. A bold idea was put into action. Outdated thinking was challenged. Cheese got moved (great book, if you haven't already read it). Or a question was asked that had never been considered before. Smell what I'm cookin'?

We'll get to the undeniable wizardry of questions very soon. I'm ignoring the ants in my pants taunting me to start sermonizing on inquiry, but, in the meantime, we're ready to combine those two words: Disruptive and Discovery. I'm grabbing a blender, sticking them in there, and turning the knob to puree.

5

UNDERSTANDING DISRUPTIVE DISCOVERY

We previously rallied around the working definition of discovery as the process of uncovering something new. After exploring the dynamics of disruption, we can put these words together and allow them to become a force to be reckoned with. The definition of this union can be upgraded by replacing "something new" with a description embodying more power, meaning, and impact.

I know the word "stuff" isn't what some folks would consider sophisticated. But I like it. All bases need covering and "stuff" checks that box for me. Plus, it's really fun to say. So, that leads us to an enhanced definition that also, coincidentally or not, is included on the cover of this book. I wonder how that happened?

Disruptive Discovery = Uncovering the Stuff That Really Matters

Or, as referenced earlier, a game changer.

To add some clarity, and a little bit of sophistication, Disruptive Discovery can be further described as *the process of gaining a deeper level of understanding with the intention of uncovering compelling learnings that motivate positive change.*

It's of paramount importance to highlight an incomparable term in that definition:

UNDERSTANDING

At the core of Disruptive Discovery is understanding. My passion for discovery is energized and fueled by an insatiable desire to understand pretty much everything I perceive to be meaningful.

The Greatest Understandings I Ever Understood

If you don't mind, I'd like to tell you a story that illustrates how an occurrence in my personal history led me to Disruptive Discovery. The event responsible for changing the high-stakes game of life for this gent is known as fatherhood.

When my Wife* was pregnant with our first child, for some reason I felt obligated to give an honest answer to anyone asking if I wanted a boy or a girl. I wasn't a big fan of the we-just-want-a-healthy-child answer either, mostly because I have yet to meet anyone who doesn't want their child to be healthy, but that's not the point. I'm guilty of stating the obvious at times, but this all-too-common response wins the blue ribbon.

Anyway, I wanted a baby girl for many reasons, so did my Wife. And I am proud to say that we were blessed with exactly what we wanted: a Daughter. Suddenly, my perspective was reoriented to a previously foreign vantage point. I began seeing everything through the eyes of a child.

As all parents know, a family expanding with a newborn challenges your status quo. Does a baby stimulate change? I'll say! All of a sudden, you realize your child has essential needs and you're responsible for doing everything within your power to keep them safe, healthy, and smiling. I had experienced Disruptive Discovery #1: *understanding what it means to be a father.*

Disruptive Discovery #2 was less than two years away. We were blessed with a second child, another Daughter.

When my second Daughter arrived, I knew right away that a roller

---

* Oh, I should address an idiosyncrasy of mine that may understandably be irritating. If you're wondering why I use a capital "W" when talking about my Wife and a capital "D" when talking about my Daughters, they aren't typos. I don't have a great explanation for it. It's just what I do. In school, we were taught that you always capitalize proper nouns. From that standpoint, in my world, there simply are no nouns more proper than Wife and Daughter. My apologies if it bugs you, but that's how I roll. Back to my story...

coaster of double trouble was waiting for me. Two girls! Priorities and purpose were rocked with my first Daughter, in the most amazingest of ways, of course. New conversations? No doubt. I was having lots of them with my Wife, friends, family, coworkers, complete strangers, and myself. As I delved into everything involved with raising *two* little girls, I took the challenge of becoming the best dad I could be to a deeper, identity-defining place. Through this self-reflection, I rediscovered myself through the uncovering of Disruptive Discovery #2: *understanding what it means to be the father, husband, and man I wish for my Daughters.*

Heavy thought? Uh, you could say that. But the onslaught of mini-epiphanies I experienced redefined the fabric of the way I saw myself in these momentous roles. Each of those discoveries were light-seeing internalizations of the responsibilities involved with raising girls in this crazy, unpredictable, and sometimes dangerous world. There are so many things out of my control as a parent, but carrying myself as a pillar in those three contexts was completely up to me. Through my actions, I could exemplify the manner in which children, spouses, and human beings in general deserve to be treated. The hope was, and still remains, that this role modeling would nourish their self-confidence and they wouldn't tolerate anything less in their future relationships with men or anyone else, or themselves. There's a happy ending to this story because my values, priorities, and beliefs about what's most important in this world changed considerably. Another often overused term is "life changing." But I can emphatically state that my life did, in fact, change. And I couldn't be more thankful for it.

An Unsung Hero

That was a little too much tissue, too early for me. And I appreciate you lending an ear through such a personal illustration. I was thinking we could now go the less emotional route by discussing a business example. This Disruptive Discovery story I feel is worthy of scrutiny as we continue connecting the dots to make the concept incredibly clear. The focus of our attention in this specimen is a little-known company, below the radar of most people. It's located in Cupertino, CA. I doubt you would have bumped into their logo anywhere, but they go by the name Apple. It's a long shot, but have you heard of them?

Ah, that's right. Apple is perhaps the company *most* benchmarked by any author trying to make a point. Apple is the epitome of a success story on so many levels. Their innovations have changed the world and you would struggle to find a company that has challenged the status quo more. After all, "Think different" was their slogan for several years.

Many experts point to Macintosh as the breakthrough technology that started a new future for Apple. It would be difficult to argue with that thinking, given the results of that product introduction and the role it played in transforming the industry. The Macintosh was an affordable, easy-to-use computer. Referring to a computer costing $2,500 in 1984 as affordable sounds a little crazy, I know. However, we can't forget that their competition was in the ballpark of double that price. I won't go into a bunch of technology details because it's way over my head, not to mention that I'm pulling out all the stops to avoid sounding uncool, so let's just agree that a ton of people now own computers because of the way Apple forced the industry to rethink everything.

Many decades later, we can point to several other Apple innovations and appreciate the way they've radically changed society. That isn't meant as hyperbole. Interaction and communication within our society has been transformed by the iPhone and the iPad maybe just a little. These are more recent examples of the way this company continues to push norms and dare the world to think differently.

However, somewhere in between those revolutionary innovations, the Macintosh and the iPhone, Apple was responsible for another industry-altering disruption. And it's one you probably don't think about very much anymore.

The iPod.

Yes, remember the iPod? I know there were many generations of that device, and it still has some popularity, but the iPod doesn't get nearly as much glory as many other Apple products. I'd like to take a minute to give the iPod some much-deserved credit. Some props, if you will. Not only because it changed the way we listen to music, but as a shining star of the way great things can happen when you uncover the stuff that really matters.

Not so long ago, people who wanted portable music had plenty of options. Apple wasn't the first to introduce this type of technology. Not even close. MP3 players had been around for years as a way to access your favorite songs while on the move. As a digital platform, the MP3 player satisfied the basic needs of consumers. Companies were competing with one another by making incremental improvements over existing models. They were trying to get better at playing the "me too" game.

Instead of following the tempting and lesser-resistance path, Apple decided to play a different game. They realized there were a few very important "what ifs" customers were expressing, both directly and indirectly, that weren't being addressed. And if the answers to those "what ifs" led to a deeper level of understanding, they could respond accordingly, so that customers would pick Apple over the other products.

In hindsight, the advancements adapted now seem basic and commonplace, but at the time, they didn't exist. They were responses to what was learned when attempting to answer a few questions that were hidden in plain sight. In essence, people were wondering, to themselves or in other subtle ways:

What if my portable music player had a better design?

What if it was easier to use?

What if there was an improved process for downloading music?

From a design standpoint, Apple went with the less-is-more aesthetic, and it worked. The iPod was a very simple device, with a sleek, hip, modern look. There weren't many buttons or things to touch. It was relatively small and could fit in your pocket, with rounded corners and a very comfortable feel. Other products on the market were clunky, not necessarily exhibiting any fashion-forward design trends.

Appearance was important for iPod customers, but what about functionality?

Apple knocked it out of the park with this feature too. Fast forward many years and ease of use is now a core benefit for all Apple products, and a major reason their customer base displays off-the-charts loyalty.

Being easy to use was certainly a hallmark attribute of the original iPod. Introducing devices that are user-friendly has evolved as a signature component of their brand and a differentiation strategy.

Not only was the iPod easy to use, it also offered an enjoyable and fun experience. It had an interface and a scroll wheel that helped in quickly finding the music you wanted. Apple incorporated the simplicity and minimalist wrinkles into their design scheme for everything, influencing the way the iPod was actually used. They resisted adding too many options. They looked at the way the device would be used through the lens of the customer and integrated only the functions essential to enjoying music. This is the age-old KISS principle, although I don't think it's nice to call people stupid. Maybe a few other names, but that's not important to this story.

Apple also eliminated a potentially significant challenge by allowing the iPod to work on PCs. Had they only allowed it to work for Mac users, they would have blocked themselves from the massive universe of Windows die-hards. Not only was this an enormous ease-of-use benefit for customers, it also proved to be super-duper savvy.

Better design and improved user-friendliness were the obvious responses to their respective "what ifs." These elevations in desirability were exemplifications of Disruptive Discovery because they were the end result of a deep-dive understanding of the desires MP3 consumers were expressing overtly and implicitly. What was uncovered went beyond the surface. But maybe they weren't the most important insights leading to the success ultimately achieved by the iPod.

Apple understood that perhaps the most compelling improvement they could make for the consumer experience was in the way songs found their way onto a music player in the first place. The process of transferring music onto a portable player was annoying at the time, when we didn't know what we didn't know about download speeds. However, this was an accepted discomfort because there was an utter unawareness of a better way being attainable. Once an improved future was made possible through the iPod, this pain point felt more painful. And a return to the Stone Age would never again be tolerated.

Not only could CDs or an entire music library be downloaded from a Mac or a PC, the introduction of iTunes opened a door for consumers that previously didn't exist. People could download songs one at a time at a very affordable price of ninety-nine cents (or maybe a few pennies more in some instances). They could get the exact songs they wanted, and only those songs, when they wanted them. Not to mention this was a completely legal option, compared to the illegal route of pirating songs from Napster. The iPod had a storage capacity for very large music libraries, and iTunes allowed people the opportunity to load it up and still be able to pay for college. By the way, iTunes was the first Apple app available for Windows, another super-duper savvy move—are you seeing a pattern here?—and further evidence of the significance of iPod in the legacy of a company that is now one of the largest in the world. Total integration was achieved and people were diggin' it.

The business model wasn't too shabby either. I mean, if you don't mind being saddled with constantly having to type so many zeros on your financial reports. Revenue for the iPod surpassed Macintosh just a few years after its initial introduction to the market, believe it or not.

By asking "What if?" Apple realized that the iPod could help consumers improve their music-listening experience in ways that mattered— really mattered—to them. In the process, the company was permanently transformed. The perception of Apple changed from that of a computer company to something much more mainstream. At the time, there were a large number of consumers who simply wouldn't purchase anything from Apple. Yes, I'm serious. That wasn't a joke. Those people indeed existed, and there were lots of them.

The reality is that, as a Disruptive Discovery, the iPod set the stage for the smartphone era. And who dominates the world of smartphones? The introduction of a little device known as the iPhone started that eruption. We can't forget that the iPhone couldn't have happened without the iPod for both conceptual and technological reasons. It laid the groundwork for arguably one of the most disruptive innovations in recent history. If I told my Daughters they could only choose one of these discoveries in their lifetime, the wheel or the iPhone, I'm pretty sure they would be just fine walking most places. More time for TikTok and Snapchat, right?

Speaking of those apps, you could point to iTunes as an instigator for the billions of dollars in revenue generated by apps on all smartphones. It opened the door for this new wave of consumer behavior. As a stand-alone business, iTunes was responsible for a king's ransom of revenue dollars. And the customized menu model paved the way for the way Apple structured their relationship with AT&T, along with the other cellular providers.

Had enough? Blah, blah, I know, I know. This long trip down iPod memory lane just keeps going and feeding on itself, but it was a necessary tie-in. The iPod can't be overlooked. And it all started with asking those two little words.

What's My Point?

I hear you and that's fair. "What if?" is a question that matters very much. We will discuss it specifically, along with other Questions That Matter, starting in Chapter 11. Had Apple not asked that question and achieved that groundbreaking understanding, who knows how the portable music industry and the future of smartphones would have developed, stagnated, or taken a path different from the way it ultimately played out?

These two examples demonstrate how Disruptive Discovery can lead to positive changes:

- A new dad learning what it means to be a parent and then redis-covering himself as a father of girls through role-modeling how they deserve to be treated in their relationships with others.

- A computer company changing an industry by uncovering the ways in which they could improve the experience of listening to music on portable devices.

In both situations, a deeper level of understanding took place. The knowledge realized was compelling. The motivation existed to arrive at a better place. A life and a company changed forever.

But how did these Disruptive Discoveries take place? What were the respective processes? How did they get started? *Why* did they get started?

I can promise you that Disruptive Discovery doesn't happen on its own. It can be difficult, frustrating, and, in some cases, painful. The end result, as these cases highlight, can be beyond rewarding. But for such benefits to become reality, an environment conducive to sharing must be created. From there, the right questions must be asked, followed by listening to the answers. This allows for an understanding of unique needs and a fostering of a desire to take action. Before any of these all-important activities become even a remote possibility, we must start at the source of so many life lessons.

Billy Joel.

6

A MATTER OF TRUST

illy Joel is awesome. Nuff said. But I will say more than enough anyway…

I've been a huge fan for most of my life, and so many of his songs from the seventies and eighties smack me in the head with a wave of nostalgia. "A Matter of Trust" isn't necessarily one of his most popular hits, but it's in my Top 10 Billy Joel Songs list for sure. If you care what I think, "Scenes from an Italian Restaurant" and "Summer, Highland Falls" are my personal favorites at an interchangeable 1–2 ranking, mood depending. Now, "A Matter of Trust" *was* his best video. No, maybe it was "Keeping the Faith." I'm a disciple. Can you tell? But I'm wholly confident you didn't come here to read about me gushing over Billy Joel, and you're probably wondering how this completely subjective yet indisputable music reference relates to Disruptive Discovery. If you insist, the title of the song "A Matter of Trust" says it all. It summarizes what makes Disruptive Discovery work, or not work, in just a few words.

I do acknowledge the absurdity of me hitching the success of this model to a love song. So, a few interpretive liberties might be required to patch up any holes. The song is basically Billy trying to convince a girl that all other relationships on the planet are dysfunctional, except theirs. No, no. They'll be together forever because they have a relationship built around trust. I'm assuming he wrote this song for Christie Brinkley, but who knows? And it's none of my business anyway. Plus, however things played out for those two doesn't take away from the sage message of the song and its overall importance. We can take the spirit of his lyrics, use them as a foundation, and apply the essential nature of trust in relationships to Disruptive Discovery.

Forget Everything You Think You Know

Trust is instrumental in the process of discovery but a *requirement* with Disruptive Discovery. One of the challenges I've found when discussing trust with others is establishing common ground on exactly what this five-letter word means. I'm not talking about the definition of trust from a website or even one of those electronic dictionaries that live in our pockets now or those old printed things that sit on a shelf. That won't get us where we want to go. I want to discuss what trust *really* means.

As I've spent time over the years observing interactions and dynamics in both personal and professional settings, I've noticed a pattern. I should mention that I'm diligent in these observations and make a conscious effort to consider the role of trust in those scenarios. When I combine those experiences with what I have learned about trust through reading, training, and from well-informed individuals, I've confidently drawn a conclusion:

Trust is one of the most misunderstood concepts in our society.

That's a bold statement, so hear me out. Trust—or distrust—is deemed an emotion by most. They direct that feeling toward others. Groups and organizations can also be the beneficiaries, or targets, of this sentiment. You'll notice a prevailing theme in each cited scenario. They all involve people. And humancentric interactions will be the focal point of our Disruptive Discovery adventure.

For the sake of rounding out the full capsulizing of trust, there are other entities to consider. For example, trust could become a factor when dealing with inanimate objects or nonhumans. Like, say, you see a suspicious-looking dog coming your way, or the weather app claims it's going to be sunny and eighty-five degrees for the trip to the beach you're planning. Will that ladder stay in place while you're cleaning the gutters? Those certainly pass muster for circumstances in which trustworthiness runs through your mind.

Regardless of the situation, trust is often used as an expression of judgment in an all-encompassing way. We hear wholesale statements such as:

"I don't trust him"

"I'm not sure if I trust that company"

"You just can't trust the news anymore"

"Don't trust that dog. Do I see foam around its mouth?"

But I'll give you the truth about trust. It's situational.

In other words, just because you don't trust someone in a particular situation doesn't mean they can't be trusted in another. The same is true for companies or groups. There are some situations in which you can place a high level of trust in the parties involved and others in which you simply shouldn't.

The weather app might be a credible tool the day before your beach trip, but we know that outdoor conditions change with the wind, pun intended, and nature-related predictions typically aren't very accurate when you're several days out. The strange dog? Yeah, maybe just stay away and work on trust once the whole foaming-mouth thing gets cleared up.

No, trust isn't a hard-and-fast judgment that can be made. And believe it or not, trust isn't an emotion. It's a decision we make from situation to situation and in different domains. That deserves redundantly repeating again one more time: Trust is a decision.

I appreciate this proposition is an acute departure from a tightly held belief. It's suggesting a realignment of what so many of us thought we knew about trust, and I can't expect everyone to agree without further thawing of the idea. If you're in the nonagreers camp, can I take a shot at swaying your thinking?

To Trust or Not to Trust

When relating trust directly to Disruptive Discovery, we should concentrate primarily on interpersonal situations. We'll walk through the procedure people use to decide their level of trust when dealing with others. That probably sounds overly robotic or rigid, but I'm trying to make strides in distinguishing trust from emotion. It's a roundabout way of saying that the decision to trust or not trust is a choice we make based on whether certain criteria have been met. Those requisites are capability, reliability, and sincerity. To take this a step further, we can run through the intellectual procedure of how we decide whether to trust someone in a specific situation. Each specific, logical requisite must be satisfied by asking ourselves the following questions:

CAN they do it? (Capability)

WILL they do it? (Reliability)

WHY are they doing it? (Sincerity)

When the answer to those three questions is "yes" or affirmative, trust can exist in that particular situation. To illustrate using a real-life scenario, think about a colleague with whom you have a strong working relationship. We can fill in the blanks so that this applies to any work-related situation, regardless of your profession. Let's assume you're working on _____ together and they're responsible for completing _____ by the deadline of _____. Do you trust them to get it done?

If they have the necessary knowledge, experience, or training, they are capable and CAN do it. If they have a proven track record or you have depended on them in the past with a successful outcome, they are reliable and WILL do it. If you feel this is something they want to do or they can benefit from achieving the necessary results, sincerity probably exists and you should have confidence in WHY they're doing it.

If the answer to any of those three questions is "no" or has a negative connotation, you might want to rethink your trust in that individual for this particular situation, even if they're someone you like very much. This is where emotion can cloud our vision and decision-making in regard to trust. And think about the ongoing debate about whether trust is earned or given. Using this questioning process, the answer is…both.

I'll give a personal example to further expound on the thinking that trust is a decision dependent on more than emotion. I can only hope this hypothetical scenario remains suppositional because it involves two things that should never be mentioned in the same sentence…my Wife and brain surgery.

I love my Wife. I feel so incredibly fortunate to share my life with such an amazing woman. She's a caring mother and heroine for our children. From a career standpoint, I would put her at rock star status, and that's only a slight exaggeration. When I hear coworkers and other professional contacts talk about her, it blows me away, and I find myself feeling so proud. What a total package she is as Wife, mother, family member, friend, and professional. As you can see, I get overemotional when talking about this special human being. And here it comes: the "but…"

As much as I love her, if I ever needed brain surgery, please keep her out of the operating room.

But wait! Why not hand her a scalpel? Didn't I just effervesce about her? If we ask the three requisite questions in reverse order, any confusion will be cleared up immediately. My Wife is obviously sincere and would do everything possible to fix my brain. Let me rephrase that, because I'm not sure my brain can be fixed, if you know what I mean. She would do everything possible to make me well. Next, I know she's reliable and could be counted on to perform the operation—if she possessed the capability. And there it is. That's the problem. She's not capable because, for all her strengths, being an accomplished brain surgeon isn't on the list.

I used this extreme illustration so we could put a magnifying glass on the inner workings of trust and why it must be disconnected from emotion.

The scope of this book isn't necessarily to thoroughly dissect and examine trust (hey, maybe that could be another book?). Instead, we're looking at trust and the role it plays with Disruptive Discovery. But, as previously mentioned, this process doesn't work without trust. Consequentially, you'll find references to trust, and its overarching importance, over and over and over and over….

To continue, we need to keep in mind that the exercise of determining trust is a two-way street. In the same manner that we're asking these questions about other people in certain situations, they're also asking them about us. We must accept and embrace this reality in the Disruptive Discovery process. This is the starting point and, potentially, the ending one, if trust can't be established.

Be Intentional With Your Intentions

Capability and reliability are often exhibited in very tangible ways. You show that something CAN be done as the first requisite. For the second question requiring affirmation, a sense of confidence can be instilled through a proven history and other indicators that you WILL get it done. However, helping someone understand WHY you're doing something to start with is a little more subjective. And this is the culprit responsible for people so often linking trust to emotion. These are often gut-feel or from-the-heart determinations.

In that context, the conversation about establishing an environment conducive to trust should really focus on sincerity. But I'd like to frame sincerity in a particular manner. When we're attempting to determine whether someone is being sincere, we're really calling into question their intentions.

There's only so much guidance or coaching I can offer about intentions. You, and only you, own your intentions. They can't be given, taught, or manufactured. It's a matter of having an honest conversation with yourself through asking, and answering, the question of your WHY.

What's the purpose of you attempting to reach that deeper level of understanding through the Disruptive Discovery process in a given situation?

The answer could be a relationship you're trying to build, a problem you want to help solve, a new learning someone wants to experience, or an awareness they seek to expand.

If intentions are coming from a good place, sincerity should be apparent. If they're coming from somewhere other than good, it will show. Maybe not right away, but eventually those intentions will become visible. The list of possible intentions falling into that bad category is very long, unfortunately. I would say that self-serving and destructive intentions would be at the top of that list, followed by many others that are undesirable, especially for the other parties involved. What about sound intentions? The good news is that's also a long list. But, again, they initiate from you alone.

Identify and own your intentions. They don't necessarily need to be grandiose or carry the weight of helping mankind. In many cases, they're reasonable and straightforward.

With that said, intentions aren't always obvious, staring us in the face or directly expressed. They can be latent or hidden and determined in a way other than someone directly communicating them to us. One of the most effective ways to reveal intentions in an indirect manner is through the basic act of being authentic. We can reach this state when our purpose is clear to us. Phrased another way, authenticity happens when we stay true to ourselves. Intentions become evident to others through our actions, just as tellingly as explicitly communicating them.

In any situation, you should look inward and explore your purpose. Have this internal discussion, potentially arguing with yourself, to get clarity about the reasons you're engaging in this process. Getting your arms around purpose is vital because it represents the core of your intentions. Look, I know this is starting to sound a little preachy and I apologize. We'll talk more about purpose in Chapter 9. In the meantime, I'm simply trying to position the relationship between our mindset and our intentions.

It wouldn't be appropriate for me to advocate specific intentions that are "good" or "bad." Intentions are formed within individuals, on personal levels, and can be subjective. With that said, in the spirit of trying to spark some ideas, here are some of the intentions I often bring to Disruptive Discovery situations in my own life. They apply to both personal and professional circles. They can be on board in either specific situations or as an ever-present influence stemming from my WHY:

- Making a positive difference

- Establishing relationships and connections of consequence with people

- Helping others find the motivation to make a meaningful change

- Teaching or coaching a new idea that will be put into action

These are just a few examples that constantly churn in my mind. Take these with a grain of salt because, once again, this is a very personal, intimate exercise. In other words, attempting to apply intentions not originating internally and organically into situations simply because they sound good is worthless, maybe even counterproductive.

Once you're well-founded in your intentions, the next step is to make them known. That brings us right back to where we started...Billy Joel and "A Matter of Trust."

No Shortcuts Here, But I'll Sell You an Express Pass

Establishing trust is the heart of Disruptive Discovery. Building trust early is essential, and it must be maintained throughout the process. Again, sincerity can be exhibited through action and behavior. Those actions and behaviors start the trust building process. But that's just the beginning. Beyond sincerity and good intentions, there are many ways to grow trust in a healthy, sustainable manner. But I'll share a little secret with you. There's one trust-building skill that's an exponential cut above the rest. And, coincidentally or not, this action has an imposing presence unmatched by most others known to man.

Empathy.

My oversimplified take on empathy is making an effort to look at situations from the perspectives of others. It's seeing things through their eyes, or envisioning how it would feel to walk in their slippers. I just realized I don't wear slippers enough and wanted to initiate a self-fulfilling prophecy. The key word mentioned is "effort." Empathy doesn't develop naturally. It takes work, diligence, and a serious commitment.

Empathy sounds like an easy concept, but it's extremely rare. I don't mean the term itself is rare; people throw it around bountifully. In fact, I sometimes cringe when hearing someone say the word because of the bordering-on-irresponsible overuse and misapplication. No, I'm saying that empathy is rare because it's so elusive. People simply aren't very empathetic in general. Its proficiency requires practice. Empathy can be developed and strengthened like a muscle.

If you take nothing else away from the time we're spending together, please make a concerted effort to practice empathy as much and as often as possible. Do you like the muscle analogy? Then join Club Empathy and start working it out. Grab some empathy dumbbells, hop on an empathy elliptical machine, or take an empathy Spin class. That's what I call committing to an analogy.

I can guarantee that more empathy will have a positive influence on your relationships and interactions with other people. And for every individual in our society who puts more empathy out there, we take one step closer to maybe—just maybe—making this world a better place.

There are no CliffsNotes or silver bullets for trust building. It's a process that requires dedication and care. But if you had to pick one takeaway, nugget, or shiny gem as the most effective tool for building trust, it's a no-brainer. Empathy rules!

Oh, and thanks, Billy. I owe you one.

7

AN EARLY INTERMISSION

haven't been to many musicals, plays, or Broadway shows. Suitably, I'm running a little low in the sophistication department, as noted by my affection for "stuff." In fact, it wouldn't be a stretch to say that I'm not sophisticated at all. But I've been to the theater on more than several occasions and enjoyed many of the performances, for the most part, in case you're interested.

Even with my severely limited expertise regarding cultural experiences, I do know that intermission is an important event. If I were being cynical—which goes against my bubbly nature—I might challenge the insertion of breaks during these performances. Is it possible, and I am merely spitballing here, that any form of entertainment lasting so long that you need to stop in the middle so you can go to the bathroom, get the blood in your legs circulating again, and mentally prepare yourself for the next act is perhaps, I don't know, too long? Sounds like a fair question to me, but it's totally feasible this is my lack of sophistication talking.

With all that sarcasm out of the way, I honestly felt like the idea of an intermission could potentially work for a book. And because this is my first attempt at writing one, I figured it was worth a shot. We can use this chapter as an intermission. Even though it seems early and we're just getting warmed up, I thought this was a perfect opportunity to recharge the battery with a brief summary of what we've covered so far. Remember, I pointed out earlier that "brief" is a relative term. At any rate, here's a roundup of where we've been and a preview where we're heading.

This all started with establishing a working definition of discovery and how it can be useful in our lives. In general, discovery expands our awareness, is involved when being exposed or introduced to something for the first time, and helps us find solutions for problems. In addition, discovery is a valuable tool in building and maintaining relationships.

From there, two types were specified: Surface Discovery and Disruptive Discovery. In our overview of Surface Discovery, we talked about the way discovery, as a process, has both similarities and differences in personal versus professional scenarios, but any overlap begins to evaporate as Surface Discovery transitions into Disruptive Discovery.

The idea that not everything disruptive is negative was evidenced. Once we got comfortable with that, we combined the two words, disruptive and discovery, causing my favorite math equation to take a quantum leap beyond simple kindergarten arithmetic. With that union, $1 + 1 = 3$ went through a metamorphosis and became:

Disruptive + Discovery = Uncovering the Stuff That Really Matters

Or with more pizzazz... *The process of gaining a deeper level of* understanding *with the* intention *of uncovering compelling learnings that motivate positive change.*

You'll notice I emphasized two words that didn't originally stand out when this concept was introduced. This emphasis can now be placed on "understanding" and "intention" because we've discussed these terms in detail.

In one personal tale I shared, *understanding* led to life-altering realizations when this dude became the father of two girls. In a less heart-tugging example, the success story of the iPod was described as the spark that transformed a company and, ultimately, an industry.

Regarding *intention*, we learned that it's evident through our actions. When intentions come from a good place, sincerity becomes apparent, and that's one of the required factors for trust to exist. Several intentions integral to my own Disruptive Discovery situations were served as food for thought.

Speaking of snacks, I could go for some Milk Duds right about now. Want some? We can head on over to the concession stand before intermission ends and grab a box. There's still much more to tell you about intentions, and that gives us a chance to keep talking while enjoying a caramelly, stick-to-your-teeth sugar rush. Then, we'll come right back to the review of our time together. I'm buying. Follow me...

Inter-intermission

To continue with the short list of personal intentions I offered, I'll say that they should help in getting your head in the game, but they were very general. You could even call them vague. Intent is a sticky concept to digest, just like those Milk Duds, so I feel the need to share one more, a smashing example. An example you're holding at this very moment, either physically or electronically.

In the first chapter, I spoke about helping people get to a better place, and the way writing this book might bring that desire to life. Yes, that's a lofty mission statement, but I hope you agree that it represents the positive intentions we strive to bring with us into trust-building situations.

What's more, these intentions are sincere because my claims are honest and truthful. But how do you, as a reader, know I'm telling the truth? That's a critical question because if you don't unequivocally believe what I profess, my sincerity is on shaky ground. That's where things get prickly, so you're just gonna have to trust me. Whoa, see what I did there, sliding in the idea of trust when you weren't looking? All joking aside, this is a legitimate and relevant dry run for us as we further inspect the linking of intention, sincerity, and trust.

If you think about it, writing a book is a pretty narcissistic exercise. It requires an author to possess the belief that they have something compelling to say. Furthermore, that author must believe readers would, indeed, want to read what they have to say. That means they must feel pretty darn good about what they have to say in the first place. The hours spent staring at a blank page, trying to fill it with words coming from muddled, disorganized thoughts can be mind-numbing. And the tenacity needed to mold and shape those words into a finished work fit to be read by someone else requires incredible self-absorption.

That, my new friends, is precisely why intentions are so important.

You would be justified in wanting to validate mine. A fair question could be posed: "Yo! Is this whole helping-people-get-to-a-better-place thing for our benefit or yours?" Now, we're really talking!

An intention doubter might point out the self-serving component of publishing a book. That's telling it like it is and can't be denied. You want people to buy it, you want people to read it, you want people to talk about it. More than likely, the book is intended to be a vehicle to help the author achieve another goal.

Is it possible to write something with both selfless and self-serving intentions? Maybe this is another one of those pesky paradoxes and maybe it isn't. I guess that depends on whether you believe there is such a thing as a selfless act. This has the makings of a great debate, and this recondite brainteaser will pop up a few more times. But for the sake of avoiding the perils of getting bogged down, I'll simply say that at the end of the day, it doesn't matter. Multiple intentions can exist in any situation. However, each must come from a good place and have something else in common. They must be sincere. All of them.

Coming back to what was posed a minute ago, I asked how you could know if I'm telling the truth about my claimed intentions, followed by the words, "trust me." Well, do you? That's a trick question. Don't answer!

If you're feeling wobbly and punch-drunk, don't worry, we're right on schedule. Trust, as a concept, is unwieldy and hard to handle. Ahhhh, if it were only as simple as following our natural inclination to associate trust with our feelings about other people and their likability, or lack thereof. To further explain why such a seemingly uncomplicated question is a trick, we must go back to our review of what we've covered so far.

As I Was Saying...

Before our detour into inter-intermission, we were revisiting how sincerity is one of the requisites that must be met for trust to develop. But perhaps my excitement got the better of me and I jumped ahead, talking about sincerity out of context. When determining whether trust exists, we must consider all three requisites. Sincerity is one of those criteria. The others are capability and reliability.

As the discussion continued, we challenged the idea that trust is an all-encompassing emotion. Instead, we needed to acknowledge the fact that trust is situational. Furthermore, with all our relationships and interactions, trust can exist in one domain but not the others. In any given situation, we must ask ourselves these questions about the people involved:

- CAN they do it?

- WILL they do it?

- WHY are they doing it?

As we know, a "no" answer or negative response to any of those questions means trust can't fully exist in that particular situation. That isn't the end of the world because, again, this is a decision driven by factors other than emotion. And in no way should it become an indictment of the character of another person. We're simply reconciling the idea of whether trust exists in a particular situation within our minds. That's the extent of the choice being made.

Building and maintaining trust happens by increasing a person's comfort level through those requisites and questions. Prove that you CAN perform a task. Instill confidence that you WILL do whatever has been committed to. Demonstrate good intentions about WHY you're doing it. Easy peasy lemon squeezy (if only).

The CAN and the WILL usually are addressed in very tangible ways. They're often obvious and apparent, sometimes even black-or-white. Things become subjective and "touchy-feely" when we get to the WHY—our sincerity—in particular situations. And that's often when some good old TLC comes into play.

What's the most effective way to build trust in the Disruptive Discovery process? That's a question without an easy answer. However, there is that singular, standout skill we pointed to as the most effective tool in building and maintaining trust...empathy. Anything else would get one of those much tinier, unsatisfying second-place trophies.

As we addressed in-depth, empathy is incredibly powerful, but it's surprisingly rare. It's a word that's often spoken but an action seldom put into practice. Empathy as a skill can be cultivated, just like a muscle. If you want to see improvement right away in building trust in various situations, try developing your empathy skills. It won't be easy, but a good starting point is simply trying to look at things through the eyes of someone else, or imagining how it would feel to walk in their shoes, or slippers. Trust will grow. You can bank on it.

What Say Ye?

We've come full circle, back to the trick question of whether you trust me. It's tricky because the answer, as we've learned, is that trust is situational and doesn't exist across the board. You can't "trust me" because we can't trust other people in an all-inclusive, whole-enchilada way.

So, I need to ask the more appropriate question: "Do you trust me *to write a book as a tool to help people*?" That question can only be answered by running it through the CAN, WILL, and WHY exercise. Am I capable? Am I reliable? Am I sincere? And I'm not allowed to answer those questions. They're for you to decide.

Trust. What a wonderful but overwhelming concept. It's at the heart of Disruptive Discovery. With trust, Disruptive Discovery is possible. Without it, Disruptive Discovery will be strenuous, if not impossible. We know that trust is situational, but the strongest relationships have lots in their foundation, just as Billy Joel told us many years ago.

How was that for a summary? I hope this fast-forward button, high-level review helped to clarify and reinforce everything we have under our belt. Next, we'll shift gears and start to get more hands-on. The following chapters represent more of a how-to guide, giving you tangible tools to get the Disruptive Discovery process started and move it forward in a manner leading to impactful results.

Uh-oh. It sounds as if I'm hearing those unmistakable bell chimes and they're doing that thing with the light dimmer. See, I wasn't lying about going to the theater. If you need to buy an eighty-dollar sweatshirt before returning to your seat, now is the perfect time. I'm still hungry because they weren't selling Milk Duds. I wonder if they have nachos. I doubt it.

This place is too highfalutin.

I guess intermission is over. You've made it this far with me. Thank you. And I promise the following acts will be even better. Are you ready for the show to start again? I am.

PART TWO

GETTING STARTED

8

FINDING THE RIGHT FIT

How are you guys doing out there? Are you ready for more? Come on! You can do better than that!

Are you ready for more?!

That crowd-enlivening routine is one of my biggest pet peeves. This happens at conferences, seminars, and social events when the person speaking tries to artificially generate enthusiasm. It's an unfortunate tragedy that turns audience members into innocent victims, when you hand a microphone to someone needing a tremendous amount of reassurance to mask their insecurities.

Sheesh. That sounded a little angry. I wonder what caused such an outburst.

It seems I should put my money where my mouth is and try some Disruptive Discovery to help me uncover what incited such unprovoked hostility. Hey, what a perfect segue! You'd almost think it was planned. Anyway, call me a hypocrite because I'm hopping on the bandwagon.

ARE YOU READY FOR MORE?!

That was exhausting. Sorry. I won't make you endure that pain again, but thanks for humoring me.

I hope you enjoyed Part One. We put in a hard day's work and I threw a lot at you. Perhaps it felt a little bit like drinking from a fire hose. We've been laying necessary groundwork by tackling some monsters: discovery, disruption, understanding, and trust. Those are all biggies and each could be a book or training program in its own right, which is the reason I felt an intermission, including a recap, was the right thing to do. There was a lot to absorb and I want to allow the learning process to take hold in a way that is both penetrating and sustainable. Not everyone has the same learning style. For some people, reading or writing is supereffective. However, others learn most efficiently through visual, auditory, or kinesthetic methods. Those techniques are obviously difficult to pull off in a nonchildren's book format. Believe it or not, I'm trying to incorporate parts of each style into this experience we're knee-deep in together. If the fire-hose comment struck a chord, it's by design, and we'll continue with more of the same.

Full-disclosure time: This chapter is going to feel like a juggernaut and I apologize in advance, but there's a lot more about to get unloaded. You've been warned.

Maybe I'm an analogy junkie because I have another one locked and loaded. Think about being on an airplane going through a patch of turbulence. Big bumps, white knuckles, and flight attendants spilling drinks all over passengers. But then the choppiness subsides and there's nothing but smooth air for the rest of the flight. That's some foreshadowing for this chapter, so stick with me.

This Is Your Captain Speaking

"There's turbulence ahead, but it will be clear skies before you know it. Just to be safe, I'm turning on the Fasten Seatbelt sign."

We've been playing at a high level, the proverbial view from 30,000 feet—I really am milking the plane analogy, huh? And that high altitude isn't a bad thing. In fact, this type of approach was necessary and to our advantage. It allowed some introduced concepts to soak in while we were getting comfortable with the different areas in which discovery could be useful. In addition, we've primed the pump for Disruptive Discovery by exploring specific examples of the impact achieved through a deeper level of understanding, another step toward our ultimate goal.

It's time to get more specific, more granular. Otherwise, it's just a lot of half-baked ideas and incomplete learnings running around in our heads with no clear indication of what in the heck to do with them. For that up-close view to take effect let's grab our test tube with everything we have mixed in it and pour that concoction through a filter. Or maybe you'd prefer a reference involving alcohol? In that case, we must distill all these fun ingredients so we can make a wicked drink. Before we start happy hour, though, it's time for an honest conversation. And this one won't be easy for me.

It's hardly noticeable, but I'm marginally enamored with Disruptive Discovery. Those big, bold words on the front cover are subtle clues, in the form of a dead giveaway, that I'm yet again using my sarcasm crutch. There's passion in my belief that this model can be used to make a positive difference in many ways. But if someone asked me to give more specifics about what I mean by the catch-all phrase, "many ways," beads of sweat might start to appear on my brow.

A Members-Only Kind of Club

You see, one of the ideals that defines me is the wishful thinking that the process of uncovering the stuff that really matters has a place for EVERYONE, EVERYWHERE, ALL THE TIME. But that's simply not realistic. If that was true, Disruptive Discovery wouldn't be so special, so powerful, so compelling. And let's be clear…it *is* special, powerful, and compelling. No, if this practice had widespread applications, it would be a commodity, like a zombie taking a knife to the head on *The Walking Dead*. (Yup, I'm still trying to overcompensate for the uncoolness I exposed with my earlier ill-advised TV-watching and music admissions.)

The truth is, this type of disruption isn't for everyone and isn't a perfect fit in all situations. This is true for a few reasons. First, Disruptive Discovery is a challenging and sometimes complex process. It requires skill to implement and effort exerted by everyone involved. Not to mention that, in many cases, reluctance or reservations could exist for any of the participating parties.

Next up, this type of discovery isn't always necessary. Unfortunately, there are situations in which good enough is…I can do this…the pain won't last long…good enough. Why do I say "unfortunately" and need to talk myself through making that statement? Because I despise the saying, "If it ain't broke, don't fix it." I prefer, "If it ain't broke, break the damn thing and make it better!" But the former type of thinking provides a sense of security for many people, and looking for a deeper level of understanding isn't on their to-do list in some situations. And that's OK, because that big, bright ball of burning gas keeps rising every morning.

Many years ago, during the early days of my career, I heard one of my mentors say, "Don't let perfect be the enemy of good enough." I thought he was brilliant and couldn't believe he was responsible for such a profound thought. Well, it turns out it wasn't his brilliance at all. In fact, that wasn't even the correct saying. The exact quote is, "*Le mieux l'ennemi du bien.*" I'm sure that version makes much more sense to you.

Pause…crickets…is this thing on?

I'm allowing a moment for that awkward silence.

Unless you speak French, I might as well be speaking, uh, French, right? Well, the literal translation goes something like, "The best is the enemy of the good." And it was originally said by the French writer Voltaire. To me, it essentially means that there's value in keeping things moving forward. Progress and momentum are tough to sustain if we stop to overanalyze everything.

But some of us are either blessed or cursed, depending on your viewpoint, with this quenchless thirst to understand, and then understand more, while trying to understand whether there's anything else that needs to be understood. We're constantly looking for those things that make a difference and then trying to determine what to do with them. Enter Disruptive Discovery.

Leveraging those two states, and getting a firm grasp on which is which, is the apex we hope to reach. Knowing when to roll with whatever momentum exists and when to pivot into higher-expectations mode is a skill necessitating intuition and judgment. The right move isn't always conspicuous. I would categorize this ability as more of an art than a science. It requires having the street-smart vision to see which situations actually present opportunities for improvement or an enhanced outcome.

With that said, I've found the most effective way to find such opportunities, as opposed to leaving well enough alone, is by looking in the places in which things are most often "broke," whether the brokenness is apparent or not. This begs the question: Which settings are most likely to benefit from the Disruptive Discovery process? The goal is to achieve maximum impact, even if that means narrowing our scope. Confused by that self-contradictory statement? It's just more turbulence and we'll keep flying through it.

The Sweet Spots

The Disruptive Discovery process, and the skills I'm hoping everyone reading will cultivate, have the greatest impact in certain environments. Want to take a guess which type? I'll give you a hint. These settings are usually multilayered, unpredictable, and often require decisions to be made. Still wondering? OK, here's another hint. They also involve *emotions*.

Aha! Situations involving…PEOPLE.

And there it is. We, as human beings, are the golden geese of Disruptive Discovery, or the gifts that keep on giving, whichever you prefer. When people get mixed up in scenarios, it's quite possible, even likely, they'll look for a way to take something otherwise intact and trample all over it just for the pleasure of making it "broke." It's as if we can't help ourselves, and much of this gravitational pull toward destruction manifests itself as behavior outside our consciousness or awareness. Human beings simply find a way to create frustration and chaos.

I don't want to give the impression of hopeless quicksand, so I think we should jump ahead to the big reveal. In an effort to get us pointed in the right direction, allow me to offer some clarity regarding how to best allocate our efforts, energy, and intentions to make a positive difference.

Disruptive Discovery is most effective when used as a tool to help people get to a better place in the following ways:

- Solving challenging problems
- Improving in development areas

This is a much more refined scope compared to "many ways." You can use this process as a means of working with people in finding enhanced solutions when problem-solving. Or you can play an important role in supporting others in determining their development areas and making the necessary improvements, personally or professionally. Ideally, you could even serve as a catalyst for them to make the necessary but difficult changes often involved in those scenarios.

Remember where we started, with a generalized summary of the way discovery could have a place in making a difference. And now we've narrowed the areas representing the best fit for Disruptive Discovery in this targeted list. As I said, it wasn't easy for me, and I'm sweating profusely.

Don't get me wrong. Expanding awareness and building relationships are altering achievements. They represent the essence of discovery, and our lives are filled with the riches of those experiences. But they often stop short of being disruptive in the ways we now recognize.

Maybe you're familiar with the term "scope creep," or maybe not. In simple terms, it's trying to be all things for all people in all situations. As you can imagine, that temptation is very real for anyone selling something. What would be a good example? Let me think for a second…hmmmm…I don't know…maybe someone wanting to write and sell a book?

Appealing to the masses is a very common strategy. You throw out a monstrous net and hope it takes in as many people as possible. The problem with this plan is the possibility of diluting the message and ultimately minimizing the potential for results. Or, in the case of Disruptive Discovery, scope creep could become counterproductive. It's difficult to simultaneously achieve wider width and deeper depth. Not impossible, but rare. There's that old saying about not being able to have your cake and eat it too. Or is it about eating only your own cake? Or you can't have someone else's cake? Don't eat too much cake? What I'm referring to is the popular figure of speech making the point that you can't have something both ways.

Cake aside, a broader scope, or wider net, for discovery leads to learnings and levels of understanding that are more surface than disruptive. As a result, this approach would, in effect, make it more difficult to help people get to a better place in the ways we've specifically identified. Look at it this way….

Would you rather help a larger number of people in smaller ways (wide) or help a smaller number of people in larger ways (deep)?

There isn't a right or wrong answer. This is something everyone must decide on their own. I do encourage you to seriously ponder that question, by the way. Really give it the amount of thought it deserves, because those two options are drastically different and a little inner-scope clarification is good for all of us. However, my gut is telling me that the reason you selected this topic for reading material and have made it this far speaks volumes.

Knowing the Audience

You might be seeing a pattern in that a particular word is all of a sudden being used over and over again. That word is "people." Uncovering the stuff that really matters happens at an interpersonal level. Helping people to solve challenging problems and improving in development areas typically happen in the realm of people interacting with other people. We need tangible tools that can be used in our business and personal environments as we engage with one another. Challenges and advancement opportunities are aplenty within people-oriented situations involving relationships, responsibilities, decision-making, and values.

All of this philosophizing and alluding is leading us somewhere. And that destination is the reality that Disruptive Discovery isn't a process recommended for everyone. Once again, there's a paradox lurking because, in theory, this method *could* be valuable for anyone. Maybe that sounds like some both-sides-of-the-mouth talking, but this is my story and I'm sticking to it.

The basis of my double-talk is that to get optimal traction and results, I'm not sure the "could" folks are the right fit for Disruptive Discovery. Expending time and energy trying to convince them to bring this technique into their regular interactions isn't something I would advocate. Not for them and not for me. Instead, the better idea is to concentrate attention on the people most likely possessing the internal fire in the belly to make a positive impact on the lives of others with this exercise.

So, I'll cut to the chase and give my perspective on who *is* the best fit for learning the skills involved with Disruptive Discovery. What profile was in the back of my mind when thinking about the individuals most likely to glom onto this ideology? What type of individual was I hoping to establish a connection with when starting this venture? Who is most likely to put this method into action? I like those questions and I've pulled together a comprehensive list meant to answer them. More accurately, these are multiple lists, but they aren't at all encompassing, accounting for all possibilities. That would be unrealistic, but this summary does cover the lion's share or, at least, enough to capture the spirit of what I'm conveying. These lists outline the individuals who are the apple of my eye for bringing Disruptive Discovery to the forefront of their interpersonal difference-making activities in professional or personal settings, or both:

Professional

- Senior leadership
- Managers or supervisors
- Sales professionals
- Business owners
- Executive coaches
- Consultants
- Trainers
- Teachers
- Mentors

Personal

- Friends
- Family members
- Individuals holding a leadership role outside their job responsibilities
- Parents
- Athletic team or club coaches
- Life coaches
- Therapists and counselors*

---

* Yeah, I went there. There is no degree, certificate, or plaque that can be earned in Disruptive Discovery, but I have the utmost conviction that it can assist with stimulating invaluable progress for patients and clients.

Both

- Advisers: Anyone who gives support to others about life or work situations, including their goals, relationships, values, greater purpose, or other development areas.

This is a relatively long combined list and can apply to a wide range of people. However, I'll say it one more time with emphasis…the process of Disruptive Discovery is *not* for everyone. There simply aren't many of us crazy people out there. (I'm referring to our brethren of maniacs constantly looking for opportunities to reach for an improved state or scoffing at the status quo. If it ain't broke, that's no fun, so please hand us a sledgehammer.)

This is why not every CEO, coach of a high school basketball team, or confidant is a natural candidate to employ this process. The fit with Disruptive Discovery is more about their disposition and motivations than whether their job category appears on this list. But the summary shows a cross section of roles that inherently involve a high degree of interpersonal activities. Those areas of responsibility also tend to be filled with a continuous flow of broken situations in need of fixing.

Because we've determined that our focus will be on situations involving people dealing with people, I should stress that sufficient levels of desire and engagement are required by everyone involved in the process. All players must be willing participants in these interactions or Disruptive Discovery will falter. This is true for both the Disruptor and the Disruptee, though we won't use those unviable terms again (I thought, just once, they might help clarify the distinct roles involved with these activities). Instead of Disruptor, let's use Facilitator of Betterment going forward.

Hold up! Stop the press! That sounds like a revolutionary new term. A facilitator in this context would be the individual implementing the Disruptive Discovery process. What do you think? I'm loving it. We should consider this a promotion and order business cards with our movin'-on-up title. Cutting out the comedy routine, though, I've given this a lot of thought and feel it's a perfect descriptor for anyone leading Disruptive Discovery exercises. Facilitator of Betterment is a lot to type, so how about we refer to this distinctive classification as Facilitator? Of course, I'll shamelessly plug the full title from time to time because I'm feeling mighty full of myself for creating such a vanguard (can you feel all the weight I've placed on my sarcasm crutch?).

Don't be disappointed, but I can't think of a better term for Disruptee that would serve as a catch-all for the different settings we've outlined. Individuals in the role of beneficiary of the process could be coworkers, customers, friends, family members, or anyone involved in the many other types of relationships with the Facilitator we outlined above. We'll refer to this role as participant, player, or stakeholder.

Did you feel that? We've flown through the turbulence and are cruising in smooth skies. The flight attendants have resumed serving mini pretzels and those addictive, molasses-infused, sugar-loaded cookies only available on airplanes. You can even keep your tray table lowered (another item not found in many places other than airplanes). We now have a clear picture of *where* Disruptive Discovery is highly applicable and *who* is most likely to find opportunities in which it could make a positive difference.

If you fit any of these descriptions and have genuine aspirations to help people get to a better place, you've come to the right…uh…place. The techniques involved can be facilitated in a manner that motivates people to explore the possibilities of embracing new, improved outcomes through positive, productive, and healthy practices. Together, you can share in those success stories and celebrations. This can be a highly rewarding experience for everyone involved.

Before the intermission, we talked about the importance of trust for this exact reason. Trust must exist in any mutually beneficial interaction taking place between people. Have I mentioned that good intentions and sincerity are requisite in trust building? Oh, yeah, to a pulp. But another component is about to be added into the mix. Those sincere intentions must be reflected in the reason you're facilitating the Disruptive Discovery process.

What's my point? Good question, but not the million-dollar one.

What's *your* point?

9

ESTABLISHING YOUR PURPOSE

lose your eyes.

Hold on! Not yet. I need to preface this activity first, and reading through closed eyelids can cause motion sickness.

It's time to visualize a specific Disruptive Discovery opportunity in your mind. In these learning situations, some people gravitate toward identifying real-life opportunities they're currently encountering as a case study. Other people operate best by dealing with hypothetical situations in which they can theoretically apply the concepts being taught. When trying to gain new skills, I tend to learn most effectively by applying both methods. I go back and forth, flip-flopping between actual scenarios and anticipating future ones, depending on the specific content. Either way, we need to begin applying principles through envisioning, and I figured the eye-closing thing was worth giving it a go.

Let's start again...

Close your eyes.

Picture an opportunity in which someone, or a group of people, wants to find a better place and get themselves there. Maybe a problem needs solving or a development area needs improving. Either way, implant this scenario firmly in your mind. Got it? Good. The rubber is about to meet the road.

We're now ready to transition into the specific steps of Disruptive Discovery and discuss how they fit into the overall process. The first order of business, as a Facilitator, is establishing your purpose.

What Brings You Here?

Think about the situation you have in your mind. Why would you initiate this exercise? What's the goal you hope to accomplish? Ultimately, once again, these are questions only you can answer. There's no app or decoder ring that will do it for you. However, that doesn't mean I can't try to lend a hand. This type of thinking sometimes needs backing, especially when trying to train our brains to think differently or engage in an activity it isn't accustomed to performing. We can get the wheels turning with a bold statement.

Mindset is everything.

And I have another gem for you as a dovetail. Our mindset is also one of the few things over which we have total control in any situation, notably those involving other people. The responsibility for bringing the necessary mindset to any interaction falls squarely and solely on one person. You.

The key is getting your mind pointed in the right direction. In simple terms, there are two primary mindsets in which the vast majority of people lean toward, depending on their proclivity for focusing attention—internal and external.

There's an easy way to define both of them. Here's what you're saying to yourself in these mindsets:

Internal = It's all about me

External = It's all about them

It doesn't take a genius to quickly realize that neither of these options is the gold standard. With an internal mindset, self-centered priorities are carried into relationships and other activities, which leads to people looking out for their own interests, even at the expense of others. Selfishness, entitlement, narcissism, and giant egos often rule in this mindset. As you can imagine, it isn't an ideal inclination or attitude for helping people.

Wait a minute. You might be thinking this is a moot point because why would someone with an internal mindset want to help people? I would offer that, in some cases, an expressed eagerness to help is nothing more than a means to an end. Unfortunately, people often camouflage an internal mindset by volunteering support. It's the with-strings-attached arrangement. I'm sure you're familiar with the term "quid pro quo." If you ever find yourself bored at a bar, party, or lame work event, I have a suggestion for entertaining yourself. Make an announcement that there's no such thing as a selfless act—there it is again—and see what happens. But think about it. Is there?

To make things even trickier, an internal mindset is easily hidden. The words people use can serve as a disguise. But, as we've previously discussed, actions really do speak louder than words, and true mindsets are eventually revealed.

An internal mindset can also be described as Win-Lose.

Equally unproductive, for completely opposite reasons, is an external mindset. In this case, the interests of others take precedence. We do whatever's possible to give them everything they want. We do whatever's possible to say "yes" and fulfill their entire list of demands. This also creates an environment of entitlement, but for the others involved. Constantly giving people what they want promotes a feeling that they should, well, get everything they want. Being taken for granted or becoming less respected are other potential byproducts of carrying an external mindset.

You're likely thinking this doesn't make sense. If the goal of Disruptive Discovery is to help people get to a better place, their needs should be our top priority, right? Right????

Nope. An external mindset represents Lose-Win.

The only sustainable outcome results when concerns or interests for all participants are fulfilled. Otherwise, you're dealing with some variation of Win-Lose (good for me and bad for you) or Lose-Win (bad for me and good for you). Eventually, one of the parties, possibly both, will decide to end their involvement in joint activities under either of these conditions if they have a choice. If the relationship or arrangement isn't optional, or it's simply too difficult to opt out, they might continue with reluctance or resentment. People will sometimes just go through the motions, and that makes the prospects of long-term success together highly unlikely.

Passive-aggressive behavior is often bred from these environments.

Oh, I should also point out the troublesome—yet very real—Lose-Lose scenarios (bad for me *and* bad for you). Unfortunately, they're out there, but that's a level of dysfunction with tires we won't even begin to kick.

I guess this is my overcomplicated way of saying that when someone is losing, it ain't good. With that line drawn in the sand, instead of putting my degree in nuclear physics to work, nothing more than levelheadedness is needed to tell us what we need to know. Simply put, Facilitators should work to avoid all mindsets involving a losing outcome for any of the parties involved. That only leaves us with one desirable option, and I'm sure you saw it coming a mile away.

Win-Win.

A Better Approach? I Say the *Only* Approach

In a mindset fixated on wins for all players, the priority is ensuring that everyone involved in the process has a feeling of security with their concerns and priorities. They must feel safe and confident that the interests most valued by them will be preserved or even enhanced. This is the consummate objective, and the only sustainable arrangement. We'll refer to this mindset as Mutual Concern. It's at the center of all Disruptive Discovery facilitations. The importance of this mindset in the process can't be overstated. In fact, I'm not sure how to adequately emphasize the prospects for enrichment that can occur in all interpersonal relationships when you bring a mindset grounded in caring for the interests of every participant.

There's another facet of Mutual Concern I've observed and find fascinating. This mindset is unnatural for us. We aren't born with the mentality of seeking reciprocal or interdependent outcomes. People are wired with either internal or external mindsets. They're inclined to look at situations as Win-Lose or Lose-Win. Adopting a Mutual Concern mindset is learned behavior, yet another skill that needs to be developed through purposeful effort.

Hold, please…

Take a breather…

Allow those ideas to percolate…

We're making headway. We've nailed down Mutual Concern as the necessary mindset for this process and acknowledge that bringing it into these interactions is within our control. This is hefty progress, but there's more. We aren't done with performing some calisthenics for the noggin as you continue to work out your own purpose.

What's Your Final Destination?

When I say that Disruptive Discovery is a tool to help people get to a better place, have you found yourself bewitched by the promise of a "better place" and wondering where exactly it can be found on a map? That's a very fair challenge of this term I've been using extensively. Maybe the best way to comprehend the way this imaginary place transitions into reality is to think of an opening.

You know? An opening. The distance between one place and another. Now, does it make sense? I'm picturing a lot of head scratching out there. A little more explanation? No problem.

I've learned that people are constantly evaluating where they *are* and where they *want to be*. The air between those places represents an opening. In other words, think about an opening as the space that exists between the Current State and the Aspirational State for any individual. If an opening is narrow, people typically feel pretty content with their situation and motivation for change might be lacking. If the opening is wide, there's usually a strong sense of urgency to try something different or make a change.

If you don't mind, I'm going to show complete disregard for the rules of writing mechanics once again and capitalize "Opening" as we continue. And, yes, it's writing mechanics and not punctuation. I looked it up. Call me a weirdo, but I think capitalizing a word makes it look more importanter. See? I got good grammar too.

Anyway, in some cases, this evaluation of states could be based on something minor or even superficial. I'll go back to the Apple well one more time and re-mention the iPhone because it effectively demonstrates the point. People rush out to buy the newest iPhone because of a perceived enormous difference, an Opening, between quality of life with their current phone and how much added happiness the newest version will bring them.

Boy, I wish that was an exaggeration and I was merely making a joke to prove a point.

On the other extreme, people wrestle with Openings in their lives related to situations carrying much more weight. Maybe it's an evaluation of where they stand with their current job compared to where they want so badly to find themselves with a new career path. Moving, starting a family, and health-related decisions are just a few other examples. Much of this appraisal is taking place behind the scenes in our brains and we aren't even consciously aware of this never-ending analysis of our Openings.

The majority of these assessments fall somewhere in the broad spectrum between trivial and life-changing. And labeling an Opening as important versus unimportant is a very subjective distinction. So often, it isn't relevant, outside of our capabilities, or none of our business. There's no need to go there. However, in the quest to establish our purpose for a specific Disruptive Discovery situation, understanding the Openings that exist for everyone involved is critical. Furthermore, the real question is whether we can play an active role in working with them to expand those Openings.

There are two ways to look at the parts played by a Facilitator in widening an Opening. One of those is to push the Aspirational State higher. Another possibility is to drive the Current State lower. Remember, we're dealing with perceptions of those two states, so this is happening somewhere within the range of conscious and subconscious awareness. As it relates to purpose, our role is to help people arrive at these realizations. A widening of an Opening occurs when someone reaches a self-understanding that the level they're striving to reach is higher, their present status is lower, or a combination of both. In short, someone becoming consciously aware of their aspired "better place" is more likely to happen as the Opening gets wider, larger, broader, more immense...you get the point.

Help Me Help You

The other component worthy of dissection regarding the way we help people get to a better place is the word "help." This is a powerful word. Scratch that. I think this calls for a juiced-up adjective. It is a *transcendent* word, and one that can take many distinct forms.

For the sake of this discussion, wanting to help people doesn't mean running into a burning building or saving a cat from a tree. This is about being a valued resource to encourage and support others in their attempts to get to a better place. Those destinations could include finding superior resolutions, acting on tough decisions, finally fixing difficulties, or committing to cultivating skills. Another mode of aiding others is by serving as a compadre in their journeys to improve areas within their personal or professional lives.

People decide to explore better solutions for problems or make developmental improvements for their own reasons. And they tend to resist such projects when those reasons originate from—are pushed by—others. This was another epiphany for me many years ago. As a manager trying to help individuals succeed in their roles, I would make attempts through various support and coaching interventions. With few exceptions, I'd find myself experiencing incredible disappointment and confusion when coworkers on my teams made only half-hearted attempts to raise performance levels in areas we'd identified together. We would schedule formal review meetings or regular conversations about achievements and put together specific plans for training or utilizing resources. Most of the time, it felt like a collaboration and we were in agreement regarding the course of action we created together. I usually found myself feeling convinced they concurred on next steps and were committed to achieving the goals established together. But the data collected from these unscientific experiments suggested that, nine times out of ten, results fell short. And I'm not merely referring to results from a performance metrics standpoint. I'm talking about behaviors and activities that didn't even closely resemble what had previously been signed off on, as if those sessions never happened. Months later, we would find ourselves either having a repeat conversation or diagnosing a new, more problematic area needing to be addressed. Why?

I have a theory. There's a shocker, right?

A lesson I've come to realize along the way is that there are two reasons people fail. They either fail because of a lack of knowledge or a lack of desire.

You can help someone gain the necessary knowledge. That can be accomplished through many different forms of learning. In my experience, that isn't true of desire. It can't be taught, trained, coached, or given. If someone wants to find, fix, learn, or build something, they'll find a way. If they don't, I'd call it a safe bet that those things will never happen. Desire works that way. People must either already carry a hunger or spark it within themselves.

But can't we inspire someone to find their desire?

Nice try. But believe it or not, you can't inspire someone. Sure, they can have a feeling of inspiration, but that's their choice. That's the misconception about many emotions. You can't make anyone feel anything. Those are choices people make, usually at subconscious levels. For that reason, two people can react to the exact same situation in completely different ways.

Ouch. There, I said it. And I'm not expecting to win many popularity contests with this thinking. As those statements continue to permeate headspace, I fully expect a line of people wrapping around the corner wanting to tell me how much they disagree with what just flew off my lips. I know this all too well from getting myself in trouble many times after attempting, unsuccessfully, to impart this wisdom to others. If you're ever looking for an argument (did I say that?), next time someone says, "You made me mad," try responding with, "It's not possible for me to MAKE you mad. You chose to feel that way." And then run away as fast as you can, because I can almost guarantee it won't be a fun conversation. Regardless, this is a fact, even if it's inconvenient to accept.

The same is true with the admirable idea of helping people. That brings us right back to my theory, and here it is...

You can't help someone unless they possess the desire to be helped.

As you explore your purpose with a particular Disruptive Discovery scenario, realize it must be matched with the necessary motivation or sense of urgency from everyone involved. If alignment doesn't exist between what you hope to accomplish and what they're willing to accomplish, your interactions will be loaded with challenges, frustrations, and the opposite of good times.

It's What's Inside That Counts

To put this in perspective, I thought it would be helpful to mention a few universal examples for different types of desires. These are sources that, in my experience, are most often behind the strong feelings people get when they want to make something happen. There are literally hundreds of them, maybe more, that you could identify for this exercise (are your eyes still closed?) but here are a few I felt would resonate the most. This list is organized alphabetically because it would be out of line for me to attempt a ranking system for anyone other than myself. I have found that people often possess a desire for:

Acceptance
Acknowledgment
Admiration
Appreciation
Control
Efficiency/Productivity
Financial (get more dough or spend less of it)
Love
Perception
Recommendation or Endorsement
Respect
Reward (giving or receiving)
Safety/Low Risk
Understanding

As you devise your purpose, you must determine whether desire is present. If so, it can be very useful to know the source or type. If not, this absence could exist for many reasons, but you probably won't be surprised by the one I'm about to mention. At this point, it's becoming an old friend.

A chapter just wouldn't be complete if I neglected to mention trust. That would feel so empty and hollow. This time, I'll be very brief and get directly to the point.

Remember that establishing and maintaining trust without positive intentions and sincerity borders on the impossible. The mindset and purpose Facilitators of Betterment bring into these interactions must reflect those good intentions along with that required level of sincerity. For that to happen, all the pieces must be integrated and coalesce in an authentic way.

I'm hoping this somewhat abstract expedition has been useful and you've successfully settled on a purpose for the specific, real-life Disruptive Discovery situation you've been considering. Or, if you're using the hypothetical approach, here's hoping you've been able to theoretically apply these concepts and feel comfortable using them in the future. Either way, clarity with purpose is critical at this stage of the process.

With the proper mindset and your specific purpose for helping an individual or a group of people get to a better place firmly established, we can begin scratching the surface of our next phase. You're about to see where I'm going with that reference.

Things are about to get really, really fun.

10

SURFACE DISCOVERY TIME...LET'S DO THIS THING!

Q uestions.

If I were paying tribute to them, my message would be short and sweet..."You complete me."

The obsession with understanding anything and everything in which I've become afflicted is reliant on questions. In this tortured world of mine (too melodramatic?), I simply can't imagine a worse nightmare than desperately wanting to understand something and not having the ability to ask those tickets to enlightenment. I'd assume that a dog who habitually chases their tail knows that feeling all too well. Not my best analogy, but I couldn't think of a better one to generate a mental picture of being smitten with something unattainable. What a canine would do with their tail once catching it will remain on the list of great unsolved mysteries, along with their plans for any car they are able to successfully run down.

How long have you been waiting for me to get on a soapbox and start waxing poetic about the mystical beauty of asking questions and how they unleash the magical potentialities of discovery? And how surprised are you that it's taken this long? You can be honest.

This deferred, prolonged placement of an in-depth review of the critical nature of questions was intentional and planned for a good reason. Because I asked you to be honest, I'll reciprocate with the same courtesy. The soul of discovery is asking questions. As mentioned a little while ago, trust is the heart. Get it? Heart and...never mind. And the mystical, magical comment was an exaggeration, but not as much as you might be thinking.

However, without the proper foundation, asking questions is the equivalent of banging your head against a wall, only causing more damage. I say more damaging because the wall doesn't feel any pain from your head crashing into it. But asking questions without first creating the necessary environment gives a splitting headache to you *and* everyone else involved.

Establishing trust, a Mutual Concern mindset, and a specific purpose puts us in the best possible position to create an environment for a productive exchange. Just know that making the commitment to burrow into and internalize those concepts was time well spent. We did the right thing by setting the table with the fancy china and special silverware. Now, it's time to stuff our faces.

As an appetizer, we'll begin by using questions as vehicles to gather information during Surface Discovery. The knowledge gained during this phase ultimately will serve as a platform for Facilitators to learn, understand, and form a basis for the deeper levels of Disruptive Discovery. The technique I'll describe needs to be carried out in a responsible and caring manner. There's a method to the madness, without the madness.

Get Off on the Right Foot

Surface Discovery requires a practical form of partnership in a cooperative, nonlegal context. All parties should have a vested interest in the outcome and the relationships involved must go beyond this-for-that. As with so many other principles incorporated in this method, the execution we'll employ is also centered in human nature. When engaging in Surface Discovery, we'll make every attempt to move this process forward in the right way, based on what we know about people, their tendencies, and how they best thrive in these settings. My goal is to outline a basic framework and provide general guidance for asking initial questions. From there, I'll make a diligent effort to instruct how we integrate the answers derived from those questions, and the information obtained, into further dialogue.

If you're wondering whether this is going to be a lesson on openended versus closed-ended questions, that's not my thing. And you won't hear me profess schemes around structuring perfect conversations, mirroring, or memorization gimmicks. I'm not going there. Those commonly taught tricks and tactics place a premium on control and manipulation. And I'll also avoid at all costs encouraging the counterproductive, yet often indulged in, habit of hammering people with question after question. That represents a very one-sided, transactional exchange of information with drastic limitations on effectiveness. It can also feel like an interrogation. When someone truly wants to interact with other participants as partners, a barrage of questions will do more harm than good.

Here comes that word again…authenticity. That's the key to the kingdom and the drum I'll continue to beat. We're striving to create an environment in which real dialogue can take place so we can truly understand the needs of all stakeholders.

Surface Discovery starts with asking the right questions. As a Facilitator of this process, the responsibility for identifying questions meeting that criteria and asking them in the proper manner is all yours. And that's no simple task. Achieving success in this exercise takes practice. It involves trial and error resulting in successes and also some bloody noses (figuratively speaking, not literally). Dedication and hard work will be required. But isn't that true with anything that matters?

There are voices in your head. I can hear them. And they're getting agitated with me. They're mumbling something along the lines of, "Thus far, you professed your love of questions, told us what *not* to do, and made things I thought were easy until a few minutes ago sound like an undertaking requiring a PhD. So, Dr. Annoying Question Guy, can you please give me a clue about how to know which questions are the 'right' ones?" Even if you weren't thinking that exact question, it's warranted and deserving of a response. So, I'll answer it.

In Surface Discovery, the questions I feel deserve the "right" description fit a certain profile. They must meet the criteria of:

✔ **Being relevant:** That means questions align with the purpose you've established. They directly relate to helping someone solve challenging problems or improve in development areas. Otherwise, you're asking questions and obtaining information not pertinent to the situation. Though irrelevance should mostly be avoided, there could be some indirect value. Feasibly, unrelated questions can assist the trust building process if they demonstrate empathy or reinforce sincerity. But numerous immaterial queries can start to have a negative effect because you can only ask so many questions before people start thinking you're being invasive...or creepy!

✔ **Applicability:** We want this type of questioning to be perceived as useful and practical. In Surface Discovery, our objective is to determine where someone currently perceives their situation and the Opening that exists, or doesn't, between that place and where they aspire to be. The Opening is essentially our baseline. Questions that are applicable guide us to that place. This means, if asked properly, our inquiries will translate into something constructive being done with the answers.

✔ **Appropriateness:** Questions must reflect the amount of trust present. Aspirational State questions typically require higher levels of trust compared to those attempting to learn about Current State. Every question has a dual function beyond gaining new information. They also gauge where we stand with regard to trust among participants. When a question is asked, you can determine if sufficient trust has been established based on the substance of answers provided and nonverbal reactions observed. I recommend investing time in studying body language. It's fascinating from a human behavior standpoint, but also helpful in these situations.

Continuing along with trust, think of the shown levels as a volume knob on a radio, or the buttons on a speaker, for the youngins out there who have never seen radios outside car dashboards. Some questions are met with a closed response, feelings of reluctance, discomfort, or uncertainty. In those cases, we must accept that the trust knob is dialed back to a lower setting and react accordingly. For whatever reason, a lack of confidence in capability, reliability, or sincerity is in play. You must put forth the effort to provide the necessary reassurances in one or more of those areas. On the flip side, a free-flowing response with little hesitation and a sense of sharing most likely means the trust knob is at the proper volume level and you can continue rocking out. We must remain vigilant regarding the criteria of being relevant, applicability, and appropriateness whenever engaging in an exchange of questions and responses.

Keeping these preconditions front of mind, it's time to talk more specifically about the kinds of questions used to acquire the information and knowledge extraordinarily valuable with initiating Surface Discovery. Just when you thought I was done with analogies, think again. I'm a little ashamed to admit that my plan was to mix things up by attempting a metaphor but couldn't figure out how to pull it off without sounding like a complete jerk. And, for the next analogy, I was tempted to keep running with the whole airplane, 30,000-foot-view thing. But, upon further review, I'm leaning toward a nonrerun comparison. Maybe something epitomizing layers. Any suggestions? Oh yeah! Good one! An onion.

Ahem. This next conversation about questions resembles an onion. Certain types of questions allow Facilitators of Betterment to begin peeling the layers and getting us further into the onion of Surface Discovery. Hope this overview doesn't make you cry.

Fire Away!

That exclamatory is superfluously cavalier, but I wanted to signify that there is indeed a rational starting point...Prerequisite questions. They're proper and well-suited for the transition from your purpose into Surface Discovery. Assuming the necessary criteria are met, asking this type of question represents a jumping-off point.

Before getting to a few recommended examples, I'd like to suggest one to avoid. For my money, "Can I ask you a few questions?" isn't the ideal way to go. That's an example of a permission question. They do have their place, but I'm not always a fan of the projected tone for this intention. Requesting permission to ask questions can create the interrogation or interview vibe we're trying to avoid. And this ask can also come across as sounding either insecure or arrogant, depending on other factors.

If possible, a meaningful connection or reference to your purpose would add to the strength of a Prerequisite question. A few hypotheticals should help illustrate the point.

- A Prerequisite question reinforcing a purpose oriented in problem-solving might look something like:

  That sounds like a real challenge for you and I'd be really interested in learning more. Are you open to talking about it?

- If the purpose you have established is aimed at a development area:

  I admire your thinking about the way performance in that area can be improved by developing some new skills. I'd really like to better understand. Cool?

There are additional benefits with Prerequisite questions, including their ability to further build trust by continuing to bolster sincerity. Do you see how these examples send a message of empathy and good intentions?

States of Affairs

Assuming the response from any Prerequisite question confirms all criteria were met, especially appropriateness, we can continue to move forward with Surface Discovery. At this point, it's important to remember that one of the primary goals with Surface Discovery is to continue refining our picture of the Opening that exists. As we know, the first component of any Opening is its Current State. We use Current State questions to take steps toward further understanding this position for people as they reveal additional insight into where they are.

The information gathered from inquiries aimed at Current State is often oriented in circumstantial details. Descriptions are likely to carry a matter-of-fact undertone. Whether they're factual or not is another issue altogether. They can also include abstract or emotional responses, often to a lesser degree. Questions geared toward getting our arms around this present snapshot can be situational in nature. They're also commonly met with a simple "yes" or "no" response. Uh-oh. The sore-spot alarm just got pulled. I'm trying to quell another minirant but can't help myself...

Contrary to most of the training that exists out there regarding how to become a question-asking superhero, "yes" and "no" are completely acceptable responses. For some inexplicable reason, avoiding questions that can be answered with a one-word affirmative or negative answer has become the be-all and end-all of conversation mastery. I take that back. It's explicable. There *is* an explanation. Predictably, my interpretation doesn't paint a rosy picture. Call me a skeptic—I prefer realist—but premeditated favoritism toward questions designed to keep the other person talking is a manipulation tactic used to satisfy an insatiable need for control in communicative exchanges. If a simple "yes" or "no" allows us to move forward in our quest for a higher level of understanding, I'll take it! Putting aside my dislike of partisanship for length of responses, the use of Current State questions helps us get a firm grip on this component of the Opening.

When looking more closely at where an individual or group finds themselves and wanting to envision where they want to be, we target this type of information through Aspirational State questions. When combining their answers to these questions with our newly found understanding of Current State, the difference between those two places becomes clear. Quantifying that disparity is the way we assess the Opening.

In some cases, responses speaking to an Aspirational State will involve facts and specific details, no doubt. Bring 'em on. But it's extremely important to get behind those answers and determine driving or motivating factors. Those influencers might reveal themselves in a more intangible manner. Beliefs, feelings, values, and other ideas involving emotions tend to have a seat at the table when facilitating a conversation with people about a better place they're trying to realize. It would be reasonable to expect a heavier dose of sharing abstract, touchy-feely ideas with these interactions.

Keep in mind, though, that, in the same way inquiries directed at the Current State are less commonly answered with long-winded responses, Aspirational State questions can also step out of character. Don't be surprised or discouraged with those horrible "yes," "no," or other one-word responses to inquiries about aspirations, even if you were hoping for more depth and detail. Discovery often unfolds off script, and we can't slip into the wrong mindset. Both questions geared toward understanding the different states will provide feedback that's a combination of the tangible and the intangible. All new information is helpful. If the questions asked are relevant, applicable, and appropriate, don't get hung up on the word count of the responses. If there's knowledge and insight involved, there's a welcome mat at the front door. Come on in!

I hope you don't mind, but I honestly feel that attempting to offer specific examples of Current State and Aspirational State questions would add limited value. There are scads of questions that fit the descriptions we've covered. A needle in a haystack comes to mind. I'm confident that a zealous commitment embodying efforts to authentically incorporate these questions into your Surface Discovery style will get you to a comfortable place.

What'd You Say? Listen Up About Listening Skills

In a perfect world, once a question is asked, you get an answer. If not, you're likely dealing with a roadblock trust issue or another obstacle that has to be overcome. Or you're talking to one of my Daughters. (That's a joke, obviously-ish. I couldn't resist.)

No, seriously, question-and-answer exchanges follow a certain protocol. The cadence resembles: ask—listen—respond—repeat. This isn't a scientific process, nor is it meant to be, but that's the generic flow.

Speaking of science, this is a perfect time to point out the disparity between hearing and listening. They aren't the same thing, and the distinction has repercussions in Surface Discovery. Referring back to the question-and-answer exchange, an ask takes place, and what happens next is key. According to this sequence, listening follows asking. If we interchanged "hear" in the place of "listen," it's the same difference, right? Wrong.

Depending on which function you activate after asking a question, the resulting information is either like gold nuggets or the rocks in Charlie Brown's trick-or-treat bag. The gold nuggets are filled with knowledge and insights. The rocks are filled with…I don't know…rock guts? Like I said, hearing and listening are vastly diverse functions. Get ready to be blown away by my mesmerizing scientific acumen.

Hearing is a biological function performed by the auditory system. Vibrations are detected by the ear and turned into nerve impulses, then travel to your brain, where they're interpreted as sounds. To be more accurate, hearing is physiology. Speaking of brains, that hurt mine. But it's still chugging along and is continuing to constantly overthink pretty much everything. You probably wouldn't be surprised to know that my little brain sees a ginormous distinction between listening and hearing.

If hearing is physiological, listening is psychological. You might want to read that sentence closely a second time just in case you think I used the same word twice. To take this thinking a step further, I believe that listening isn't just psychological but also behavioral, and yet another learned skill requiring cultivation. Hearing gets the words from another person into your brain. But listening is what happens to those words once they get inside your brain. Rewind back to the bad joke about my Daughters…I know they *hear* me, but it's debatable how much *listening* goes on.

A cynic might say this is nonsense. If you want to get better at listening, duh, it's not that hard. Just pay attention to what someone is saying. It would be difficult to argue with that approach at face value. The problem exists with the well-intended pursuit of paying attention and how it works in practice. There's strategy and technique involved in obtaining information or data and translating it into functional knowledge. One of the concepts to help us with this skill is Attentive Listening.

Yes, we must give our attention when listening attentively. That's the ante you up to get your cards. The know-how involved is the ability to focus that attention in the optimal places. As information from someone is being received, you listen for specific things, especially anything that refers directly to where they are or where they want to be. We must remain observant while watching the radar for any direct or implied details relating to challenges, needs, problems, or changes, just to name a few. When this type of exchange happens, information can transform into knowledge or, even better, insight.

Another concept that appears obvious on the surface but requires purposeful effort is Interactive Listening. In simple terms, you stay actively engaged while another person is talking. Active engagement isn't code for interrupting in midsentence to show off your stirring ingenuity. And having that look on your face with your mouth half open, letting the other person know you're waiting for them to pause so you can get out the words that have been burning a hole in your tongue doesn't pass either. We're all frequently guilty of that crime, so don't even pretend to think you're the only one immune to it. Instead, Interactive Listening is a way to create a supportive, safe, comfortable environment through verbal and nonverbal communication. This is a way to engage while listening and, as a result, encourage the other person to continue sharing. It might sound a little like one of those tricks or tactics we've been fending off, but I promise, that's not the case.

Interactive Listening can be done in an authentic manner. If someone says something interesting, you can respond with, "That's interesting" in a nonintrusive way. If they say something surprising, those comments could get met with a "Really?"

Another concept that supports this type of interaction is the use of Clarifying questions. These can be potent when making a concentrated effort to listen interactively. If you're confused by a response, a Clarifying question of "I don't understand?" might be warranted. When processing feedback that's either complicated or disjointed, don't hesitate to ask, "What do you mean?" or "Can you explain that for me?" You get the idea. These are verbal cues advertising that you want to hear more.

The same message can be transmitted by connecting nonverbally. This form of communication takes place effortlessly when interactions are rooted in authenticity. If genuinely interested in what is being said, eye contact happens naturally. And the nodding of your head, or the look on your face, or the forward lean into the conversation lets others know that you're listening, learning, and striving to gain as much as possible from them. Want to practice? Show me your confused face. Just kidding.

That's how effective listening happens. Once we, as Facilitators, ask questions, Attentive and Interactive Listening concepts are utilized as answers are being received. Think of listening as absorbing information.

I was a frat boy in college and my pledge nickname was "Sponge," if that tells you anything. We listen and then respond with either additional questions or supportive comments. Then the protocol repeats itself, using the same cadence. This leads to a healthy back-and-forth: ask—listen—respond. And responding requires talking.

Damn. That's a trigger for me. And right when we were getting into a groove! We interrupt this regularly scheduled program to bring you yet another tirade…

I'm sure you've heard the adage educating us on the greatness of having two ears and only one mouth. And what about the weird game some people play in meetings, when they're intentionally silent as they wait until the other person talks first. If that ridiculous contest doesn't already have a name, I would like to submit a nomination.

Bullshit.

What do you think? I say it's a perfect moniker for a tactic that's very calculated and, again, very manipulative. Yes, the tricks people are taught, at work and in their personal lives, to seize control of interpersonal communications horrify me more than a little. Regardless, I'm not sure when talking became evil. And why someone would make such an effort to not speak during a conversation…a freaking conversation…makes no sense to me. No, the problem isn't talking. The problem is WHAT people say, WHEN they say it, HOW MUCH they say, and WHY anything was said in the first place.

Which brings us back to how communicating, verbally and nonverbally, is essential during Surface Discovery. Communication, including talking, is a tool required for asking the necessary types of questions and enhancing effective listening skills. I think we covered it pretty thoroughly. Sorry, horse. No more beatings. You can rest in peace.

Running *Toward* Disruption

At some point, once a critical mass is reached with learnings gathered from Surface Discovery, it's important to articulate our progress and begin to transition into the next phase. How? By using a two-step exercise.

First, we provide a recap of the Opening. Such a summation would essentially consist of an overview highlighting the elements we learned were discrepancies between Current and Aspirational States, combined with the growth that can be attained by addressing them. Next, follow with a question that allows for confirmation or some form of disagreement. Boom! What a powerful, compact package!

Recapping the Opening in this one-two punch format provides an informal review while serving several other necessary functions. It ensures that, as Facilitators, we're on the right track, the same page with everyone involved. An opportunity is created for buy-in to ensue or adjustments to be made. It reinforces empathy by demonstrating listening and understanding. To continue down the trails we're blazing with different purposes, maybe imagined illustrations would offer guidance on how to express recaps:

- **Problem-solving**
  After thinking about everything you've explained, I now understand the challenge you're facing. It sounds like the problem you'd like to address is _____. And if you could find a better solution, the benefits would be _____. Does that sound accurate or did I miss any details?

- **Development area**
  I really appreciate you sharing so much about wanting to make some significant improvements with _____. If I'm properly comprehending the situation, you feel developing a higher level of competence in that area would allow you to _____. Do you agree? Would you add anything?

For the next step, we grease the skids for ourselves to continue directly into Disruptive Discovery. This is done through a Transition question to move us deeper into the process. This brings us somewhat full circle in a spectacular way. We can go back to the starting point, when I described Disruptive Discovery after combining those words for the first time:

The process of gaining a deeper level of understanding with the intention of uncovering compelling learnings that motivate positive change.

We should view transitioning into Disruptive Discovery through the lens of those distinct, but related, outcomes:

- A deeper level of understanding
- Uncovering compelling learnings
- Motivating positive change

Transition questions err on the side of the forthright. They represent a gut check for an individual or a group. We've reached a crossroads of either making the necessary commitment to continue or choosing another route. The specific question asked should directly address what needs to happen next for results to be achieved:

- Is there a desire to take a dive into deeper levels of understanding?
- Do they want to attain learnings that are compelling?
- Are they feeling motivated to make a positive change?

There is only one way to find out. Forge a Transition question in your own words. Or, depending on the situation, the transition could be a combination of several questions.

Trust check time! After asking your Transition question, you'll quickly get a sense of its appropriateness. What does the trust knob read? At a high setting, you're good to go. If it's dialed to a low number, or even in that lukewarm range, you need to invest the necessary time and energy to build trust before going any further.

This has been a stout chapter, I know. I get all kinds of revved up talking about questions. As a refresher, the goal of Surface Discovery is to establish a baseline for the difference that exists between Current and Aspirational States. We're working with people to help them acknowledge where they are and to get them envisioning where they'd like to be. In other words, as this Opening becomes consciously visible, there's an awareness that a better place exists and can become a reality. The transition into Disruptive Discovery begins to expand that Opening. As it gets bigger, so does the motivation to make a change.

How do we expand the Opening and make it even more open? Once again, questions will be used as a tool for focusing on what's important. Allow me to push the envelope further...

We'll use special types of questions as disruptive dynamite to blow the Opening wide open, exposing what's most compelling.

THE STUFF THAT REALLY MATTERS.

PART THREE

THE 10 QUESTIONS
THAT MATTER

11

PRELUDE

As a rookie, wannabe philosopher, I can only dream of coining one of those phrases that lasts for centuries. Just like Aristotle, Socrates, and Plato. Perhaps that's a little too ambitious and a harebrained goal in the first place. As an alternative, how about a quote I just hatched for our burgeoning clique of Disruptive Discovery enthusiasts: *To uncover the stuff that really matters, we must ask the questions that matter.*

That could be our motto! Ignoring the comic relief, do me a favor and read that sentence again. Pretty please? I wouldn't ask if it wasn't really important. All done? Thank you.

For the next ten chapters, we'll explore the 10 Questions That Matter. These questions will be our trusted companions after the transition in our process from Surface Discovery to Disruptive Discovery. And if you're trying to catch me in a misuse of trust, I'm using it properly because each of these questions have passed the requisites with flying colors.

We'll cover each question by answering these four...uh...questions:

- WHY does it matter?
- WHEN does it matter?
- HOW is it asked in a way that matters?
- WHAT are some examples of it mattering?

The Questions That Matter aren't meant to serve as tactics or tricks— not at all. As mentioned earlier, authenticity is preeminent and not going anywhere. Remaining authentic throughout Disruptive Discovery will be an ever-present theme as we go forward together.

For what it's worth, picking ten questions wasn't part of a master plan or some evil-genius marketing strategy. Yes, Top 10 lists are very popular and make for a nice, neat package. Without such lists, we'd need to find a new excuse to make abundant quantities of T-shirts, coffee mugs, and customized knickknacks. Come to think of it, I could use a new mouse pad.

The fact I selected a round number of ten questions is a coincidence. I pinkie swear it. My love for questions is well-documented and I'm not about to start playing hard-to-get now. Right or wrong, I've tallied a ridiculous number of them in both professional and personal settings. Most importantly, I have listened to the responses. Based on those experiences, I can say with a high level of certainty that there are only a limited number of questions that truly lead to really mattering answers. It just so happens I believe there are ten of them.

On that note, I'm dropping the microphone to end this crazy short chapter. I just can't wait any longer for where we're going next. It's time to get disruptive. The stuff that really matters is waiting for us.

12

QUESTION THAT MATTERS #1

WHAT IF?

A s I anxiously began writing this first chapter of diving into the
Questions That Matter, a sneaky dilemma previously lurking in
the shadows was now staring me down. Where to start, where to
start? I found myself tussling with intense confliction, but in the best kind
of way.

I fancy myself an aficionado and a self-certified (to be clear) subject
matter expert of questions. Hey, what can I say? Because there's no such
official designations, I can assign them to anyone, including me. Because
of this honor I have so graciously bestowed upon myself, I'm now holding
a knife that cuts both ways. In one way, getting to the point of exploring these ten wonders slices through like Christmas morning. A familiar
feeling was rekindled, as I thought about this milestone more and more.
I began recognizing the same giddiness felt as a young child when seeing
that pile of presents for the first time on Christmas morning. But on those
never-to-be-forgotten mornings, giddiness quickly turned into paralysis
for a little kid facing a big decision…the other side of the knife.

Which one do I open first!?!?

Needless to say, that feeling didn't last long. Within minutes, maybe
seconds, all the gifts had been ripped open and my family was swimming

in a sea of wrapping paper destined to either overflow a landfill or put some ozone-depleting fumes into the air after burning that heap in the fireplace.

In the abovementioned predicament, the other side of the knife represented an equally wrenching choice. Which of the Questions That Matter should we tackle first? It had a similar no-win connotation as when my Daughters ask who I like best between them.

Speaking of kids, there's little mystery surrounding which question most of our adorable, innocent friends would put in the top spot. Beyond a shadow of a doubt, it would be a question starting with "Can I have...?"

Tangent. My fault. Back to my story.

The good news is that this agonizing decision wasn't about picking a "best" or a "favorite" question. As we know, that wouldn't be possible because it would depend on the specific situation. My quandary was determining which one would be used for our inauguration ceremony. Instead of choosing sides, I decided to begin with the question we've already discussed in our journey together.

"What if?"

In truth, "What if?" is an incomplete question. Those two words standing on their own lack the necessary context and direction. With some assistance, they'll be able to thrive. In practice, the question would look like:

"What if _____?"

Are you digging the recent flurry of fill-in-the-blanks? Makes me want to play Mad Libs. But we don't have time for word games. I'll explain how we fill the blank space momentarily. Without any further ado, let's breakdown our four questions in regard to this question.

WHY *DOES IT MATTER?*

When utilizing "What if _____?" we're encouraging people to think about hypothetical outcomes. They can envision a glimpse of the future by predicting how certain possibilities or ideas would play out, assuming they become a reality. This approach is intentionally open in nature and allows for a wide scope of answers. The ideal responses resemble what you might get when mixing two cups of an educated guess, a tablespoon of brainstorming, and a pinch of experimentation. A "What if _____?" query fosters safe and comfortable climates as we encourage people to visualize outcomes in a risk-free manner. It's like a mental simulation or practice shot.

There's another variation of a "What if?" question that's fundamental in our synopsis. This version is an exercise in exploring the relationship between actions and their consequences. We know this principle best as cause and effect. Typically, these correlations are conveyed as statements, though when used in question form, they morph into a very constructive opportunity for anticipating how potential scenarios might unfold under certain conditions:

"If _____, then?"

This might initially read as a subtle difference in the way we can put the word "if" to work. But even a seemingly minor twist can lead to undoubtedly distinct results. When using this version of the question, it transforms into a cause-and-effect probe. The resulting answers tend to shift broader hypotheticals into a more deliberate or pointed framework. Either adaptation of the question will elicit motion and move the needle, one way or the other.

WHEN DOES IT MATTER?

As we will see with many of the Questions That Matter, timing is everything. This exercise of considering hypotheticals is most effective at the time in which different options are materializing or evolving. When decisions or alternatives are becoming more tangible, they can often benefit from a form of vetting. Maybe it's an innovative idea that needs to be confirmed to keep pushing it forward. Or perhaps it's a long shot, a flier of a whim that will be a time and energy drain until taken off the table.

"What if _____?" is best incorporated into the early stages of exploring preliminary thoughts or formulating courses of action.

"If _____, then?" is most timely when further along in the consideration process. It puts someone in a position to envision a more specific future outlook.

If asked prematurely, before a potential option has emerged as viable, people might find it challenging to think about hypothetical outcomes in a realistic way. On the other extreme, when asked at a point too far down the road, those involved can become attached to ideas, even if they clearly aren't winning any blue ribbons. For the gamblers out there, this is known as being pot committed. As with so many interpersonal dynamics, knowing the right time is a gut feel, but these hints should serve as a guide.

HOW *IS IT ASKED IN A WAY THAT MATTERS?*

I have good news and bad news. Which one do you want first? Because I'm an incurable optimist, with incurable sarcasmitis, I say we should lead with the good news. In theory, changing the status of this Question That Matters from incomplete to complete isn't a daunting undertaking. In our fill-in-the-blanks exercise, you simply finish the question by inserting the options being examined in the empty space.

For the bad news, watch your step, because there's a paradoxical bear trap hidden out there. Yes, you're posing the question by fulfilling the emptiness of a blank space. The words are technically coming from your mouth. But they can't be *your* words. The ideas, choices, assumptions, or decisions being envisioned must originate from the individuals you're leading through this process.

With regard to how we actually fill those blanks, the verbiage used in both forms of a "What if?" question must be action-based. If we want to talk in grammatical terms, there needs to be a verb involved. You're asking to anticipate or imagine what would happen as the result of something taking place. This is pretty straightforward in the "What if _____?" format. You simply insert the action-based scenario in the blank.

However, for "If _____, then?" you'll notice there isn't a second blank space. This was intentional, not an oversight. You can consider it another one of those method-to-the-madness things. In this model of the question, "then" has lots of flexibility and can move in a number of directions. It's not the literal, Mad Libs–style filling in the blanks. Putting an individual in a position to articulate the "then" is absolutely, without question, an action-based, envisioning process, with a smorgasbord of possibilities at your disposal.

I'm sure some of my unrequested elementary school grammar lessons are irritating, but are you ready for another one?

I've never been able to say that grammar was one of my strengths. Once I started this writing project, I quickly realized I'm pretty much a grammar idiot. An unintended, yet welcome, benefit of the experience has been learning several grammatical nuances. And I figured the least I could do for my readers is to pass along some of my freshly instilled literacy riches. You're welcome! So, here's today's lesson…

Auxiliary verbs.

These are helping verbs and must be used in conjunction with main verbs. And they're perfect candidates to be used in a "If _____, then?" question. Some commonly used options are would, could, how, and should.

Using an auxiliary verb combined with an action-oriented verb is an excellent choice as a replacement for "then" in this form of the question. It's useful in helping someone consider a specific cause-and-effect scenario. Don't let the grammar talk intimidate you. In the following section, you'll find a few illustrations of how this combination might look in practice. From there, give it a shot. Maybe you could earn a sticker or a gold star. OK, enough of the schoolteacher routine. Class dismissed.

In addition, considering possibilities through the "If _____, then?" exercise is more direct. The blank is filled by a hypothetical action (cause) followed by asking about the anticipated result (effect) through an aptly applied auxiliary/action-oriented verb combo. As mentioned earlier, cause and effect is most commonly presented as a statement. You're telling someone what will happen or already did. But in our facilitation process, that would be kryptonite. This is one of those times when it would be prudent to turn the tables so that you can do more listening than talking. By asking for the predicted effect in question form, you're allowing them to complete the statement. These are their thoughts, not ours.

Finally, as a Question That Matters, "What if?" can be used as a technique to think about multiple options. When asked using multiples variables, both versions can serve as an effective way to anticipate or con-template the potential of those options. There are two ways to make that happen as a Facilitator. You could fill more than one blank in this manner:

What if _____ or _____?
If _____ or _____, then?

If those question designs seem overpowering in a particular moment, the other approach would be to simply use the standard format as many times as necessary to cover all scenarios being considered. Just make sure the exchange doesn't devolve into a rapid-fire interrogation.

Nah, no worries here. I have faith this would never happen because of the Interactive Listening skill muscles you've been building.

WHAT ARE SOME EXAMPLES OF IT MATTERING?

I already mentioned that this question was no stranger to us. Not long ago, we toured the halls of technological innovation by spotlighting Apple as a case study for effectively utilizing their own version of a Disruptive Discovery process to gain deeper levels of understanding about the needs of their customers. As a result, a game-changing innovation, the iPod, trans-pired. I'll preface the upcoming assertion with more full disclosure. Not that you suspected otherwise, but, just in case, I've never worked for Apple. I have a hunch my application wouldn't make it past the first screening, and rightfully so. Not that you thought otherwise, but I certainly wasn't privy to anything discussed in the meetings of the head muckety-mucks during the time when the iPod was being imagined. However, based on what we know about the value proposition that was delivered, I'm quite certain Apple was asking the following Questions That Matter to MP3 consumers directly and indirectly, using different words or just listening to the market using their unrivaled intuition:

What if *your portable music player had a better design?*
What if *it was easier to use?*
What if *there was an improved process for downloading music?*

Notice anything familiar about those questions? Right on. They all start with "What if _____." These are also fitting examples of how this version of the question could be used to understand whether any of those features would lead to a better place for customers.

Sticking with the same case study, we can ask these questions using the "If _____, then?" variation. The spirit of each question is very similar, but pay close attention to how the cause-and-effect wording mechanics, using auxiliary/action-oriented verb combos, steer toward a more specific, focused response:

If *your portable music player had a better design,* COULD it become a status symbol?

If *it was easier to use,* HOW does that change the ways you listen to music?

If *there was an improved process for downloading music,* WOULD you purchase more songs?

Christmas morning is off to a good start. For my choice of which present to open first, I went with the one that most kids would pick…the biggest one! I would say that "What if?" fits that description. Not so much with word or consonant count, but more from a conceptual standpoint. It's a supersized question to grasp and master.

Let's see…which one should we open next? I often hear people say that the best gifts come in small packages. I'm tearing into my stocking to find out.

13

QUESTION THAT MATTERS #2

SO WHAT?

Other than the cross-examination-like line of questioning used to badger presumably unwilling witnesses when impersonating an attorney in the ongoing trial of Snavely vs. Pumpkin Pie, "So what?" and I are the most inseparable. He's my sidekick. Or maybe I'm his sidekick. Her sidekick? Their sidekick? Regardless, we've spent a lot of time together. If that question had a rewards program, I'd be in at the mack daddy tier. And I don't discriminate between personal and professional settings when pulling the trigger on this question. It has wear and tear in all stomping grounds.

People often speculate about what their tombstone will say. I have a feeling one day there'll be constant double takes happening in the cemetery in which I'm resting as perplexed visitors pass my plot. Often heard comments might sound like, "Boy, everyone must have thought he was an awful human being. They put 'So what?' on his tombstone."

This question is small and mighty. There are no blanks to be filled in. The entire question is only two words long. I should mention that it has a few close relatives that are equally direct and stingy on word usage:

"Who cares?"

"What's the point?"

"Yeah, and...?"

These variants are effectively one and the same, but used in different applications.

And aren't they just delightful? As you can imagine, such zingers really make people feel warm and fuzzy. Welcome to the house of horrors I call home. Come sit by the fire and feel my pain, I mean, get comfortable.

No, no. Come back! Don't run away! It's not that bad. I'm exaggerating, cough, cough, for dramatic effect, cough, cough. Though I'll say without hesitation that if you're looking for a surefire way to rouse the disruption in Disruptive Discovery, you've come to the right chapter. And I'm glad you could stop by.

Out of context, you could look at those two words, or any of the variations, and say they appear to be provoking a confrontation. But in context, when asked with care and in a manner consistent with our positive intentions, they can help facilitate much-needed introspection. Here's a little secret…

There are more amiable ways to ask, "So what?" or its kinfolk at the family reunion, without using such biting verbiage. Fortunately, those alternatives won't entice people into breaking something over your head.

WHY DOES IT MATTER?

Before delving into the different forms of this question, we need to get clarity on the beneficent purpose of an approach that appears unduly bold to the naked eye. It can lead to another rubber-meeting-the-road moment of truth. This Question That Matters will cut through any nonsense like a machete and acts as a bare-bones vetting exercise for ideas, decisions, or proposed solutions. When posing "So what?" in any of those scenarios, we're challenging their relevance, substance, or potential for impact, possibly all the above.

Another function of this question is to serve as a filter for new information obtained. It can be used as an expression of tough love by pushing back on any assumptions about fresh knowledge, even if it appears groundbreaking. There's often a temptation to presume novel takeaways are difference-making insights. Different doesn't always equal valid or grander prospects. In many cases, different is simply different, and thinking otherwise can lead to future cautionary tales.

Without putting this challenge on the table, significant time can be wasted pursuing options that aren't in the best interests of all stakeholders. Presumably, they would eventually fall by the wayside or, much worse, be implemented.

On the most no-frills level, this type of question matters because it forces all players involved in the process to take a hard look at what matters.

WHEN *DOES IT MATTER?*

The point at which a determination is being made on whether an idea, decision, or proposed solution will make a definitive contribution is "So what?" time. In other words, you would need to determine the place in your facilitation process at which passing judgment is not only acceptable but a necessity. This is the validation stage. Everyone involved must affirm whatever is being considered as worthwhile, consequential, and substantial enough to proceed. Does it have meaning beyond just sounding good or feeling right?

When being used as a filter for new learnings, this form of questioning should be performed when the assimilation of concepts surpasses superficial curiosity. Not all information obtained is owed further consideration. As certain intelligence or data is received, there's value in confirming merit as it relates to the issue at hand. Otherwise, that information can muddy the waters unnecessarily and ultimately slow or confuse the process.

In uncomplicated terms, the ideal timing for this question of corroboration is before a shift from the conceptual to reality takes place. There's nothing wrong with noodling. But not all noodles have what it takes to become fettuccine Alfredo, or whatever pasta dish you prefer.

HOW *IS IT ASKED IN A WAY THAT MATTERS?*

The best advice I can offer is to be careful. To realize the tremendous benefits involved from this question, Facilitators of Betterment must assume some risk. In many ways, asking "So what?" is like walking a tightrope.

Without the appropriate white-glove treatment, recipients might sense disagreement or insinuation, or that they're being declared in the wrong. If we're genuine in our established purpose, that perception would be a misinterpretation. We know our interests are to challenge in a productive manner and provide an opportunity to either reinforce thinking or realize adjustments need to occur. But do *they* know our intentions? If not, any of these questions could be viewed as nothing more than looking for an argument (is it just me or do I mention argument-seeking too often?).

The specific words spoken in the chosen iteration largely depend on something that only you know and control about yourself. That something is known as personality.

I can't help you much on this slippery slope. Personalities are very personal because...they're personalities. We own them completely and need to have self-awareness about the way people perceive our actions. Personalities manifest through the behaviors we demonstrate during interactions. We can adapt them to different situations. Call it style or demeanor, but this is basically our portrayal of ourselves to others.

A word to the wise: Offering suggestions to anyone about their personality isn't recommended. It's a web I try to avoid flying into, and if I somehow get myself trapped in such an awful misstep, I fully expect anyone within earshot to remind me of the incredibly fragile glass house in which I live.

Along those lines, I'm pretty comfortable directly asking "So what?" or "Who cares?" simply because that fits my style. Is it always the right call? Absolutely not. There have been many situations in which I needed to adjust that style or demeanor because of the level of trust that existed—or didn't.

With "So what?" *you* aren't passing judgment or making a justification...*they* are. You're simply the catalyst. Exercise plenty of awareness about any intimation or inferences you might be giving off, calculated or otherwise, and how they're being perceived. It's a piece of cake. Just like walking a tightrope.

Next on the docket, we should pull together some representations of phrasings for this Question That Matters. As we lay them out, remember to keep our conversation about personality in mind. Give thought to the way your style might be infused in these prototypes.

Ever get one of those surveys after a conference, seminar, or training session? You know the ones I'm talking about. They ask about the venue, the food, the speakers, and whether there were cool trinkets in the swag bag. Maybe they ask whether you'd recommend it to a friend or colleague. And they usually end with the dreaded, giant open space asking for suggestions.

All of that is fine and dandy, I guess. But what happens with the answers? Nothing. Well, that's not entirely fair. They probably get circulated among the meeting planners, after which there's a flurry of defensive conversations about any low scores or negative comments. But nothing significant happens. I should add a disclaimer: Nothing significant happens *in my experience.*

I wouldn't categorize many questions as completely worthless, but the questions on most surveys look, swim, and quack like that duck, as they say. Not wanting to lodge a complaint without offering a solution, as an alternative, I recommend to any survey creator the following question twosome:

What did you learn?
What will you do differently with what you learned?

Following the completion of any events, educational programs, books, or self-development exercises, those are the only questions that are relevant and actionable. And I don't offer this suggestion as baseless speculation. That pair of questions is beloved to me and I use it inexhaustibly, practicing what I preach. Using them in combination represents a much more affable expression of "So what?"

The first question is a harmless way to show curiosity and obtain tangible feedback. The second could potentially be received with more resistance. Defensiveness might flare up because you're putting someone in the position of informally committing themselves to action, change, or next steps. Relatively speaking, such a reaction would measure as a scaled-down reading on the confrontation scale, but it's still worth noting.

What about the customer satisfaction questionnaire that's sent to your e-mail address after an oil change? They ask you to rate your experience on a 1–10 scale and give you a chance to fire off some passive-aggressive complaints. After running these questionnaires through our Sowhat-izer machine, we can take a stab at revamping this type of post-sale customer communication:

You visited us today with specific expectations.
In what ways did we meet those expectations? _____
In what ways did we fall short? _____
Please know that we will contact you immediately to resolve any dissatisfaction with your experience.

Obviously, you must walk the talk with that type of promise. Don't commit to follow-up unless you can make it happen. And surveys aren't the most effective mechanism for collecting this feedback, by the way. Burdening a customer with taking time to write responses not only diminishes the effectiveness of the exercise, it can also be viewed as an insincere annoyance. If the oil change company wants to genuinely solicit input, they should have an employee ask me while I'm killing time in the waiting room, perish the thought.

For some examples outside of surveys or questionnaires, let's assume you're collaborating with a team of coworkers to review an idea they think could lead to "breakthrough results" for your project. Here's a question to ask:

What would be the measurable impact to our company?

Or maybe you're working with a customer and have offered a solution to their problem. They respond with an apprehension that wasn't previously expressed and doesn't appear to have a direct connection to the needs you discovered during the process. Such objections are often red herrings or an attempt to stall and can be handled in this manner:

That's an interesting point I'd like to better understand. I'm wondering about the specific role your concerns would play in the problems we're trying to address together. Would you be willing to explain?

Perhaps you're coaching an individual with a competence area they have decided to improve:

What particular beneficial results do you believe will be experienced with advancing that skill?

A common scenario that often needs a healthy dose of "Yeah, and...?" is with new learnings. Just because we come across previously unknown information does not mean it will grow legs and start running. If you were working in a consulting capacity, officially or informally, maybe the following inquiry would be reasonable after someone shares a takeaway they have obtained:

It appears that this new trend in the market could lead to significant changes for the demand of your product line. With this information in mind, what are your thoughts around what gets done with it?

In our personal relationships, how often do we deal with close friends or family members looking at making that epic decision guaranteed to bring them joy and happiness? Because, you know, all it takes is one life-altering change and we'll spring out of bed every morning into a euphoric paradise for always.

I acknowledge my ceaseless use of sarcasm, but this sounds a little too familiar, right? Here's a peek at how we could use an expression of this Question That Matters as a means to promote self-reflection for someone confiding in you and seeking advice on a career move they're considering:

*You sound really excited about the possibility of that new job oppor-
tunity.* Just curious about the positive impact you think it will
bring, compared to staying the course on your current path.*

If you strip any of these examples down to a bare minimum, essentially the question being asked is, "So what?" And sometimes, depending
on your style and the amount of trust in the air, that's the exact question
that should be put out there.

Before moving on to the next Question That Matters, I couldn't resist
this final illustration. Have you ever been forced to miss the "biggest party
of the year"? Or maybe you've lived this dilemma vicariously through your
kids, friends, or professional contacts. Next time you encounter such a
tragedy, once the Fear Of Missing Out (FOMO) cloud clears—which
does not discriminate in terms of age—ask yourself, or someone else, this
compassionate and delicate question...

Who cares?

---

*I should mention that "job opportunity" is interchangeable in that example. Try replacing it
with "hobby," "boyfriend/girlfriend," "pet ferret," or any other item representing a significant
life change.

14

QUESTION THAT MATTERS #3

RANGE-FINDING

No, the chapter title doesn't mean I'm going to start talking about guns. Wrong book.

We live in a society engrossed with extremes.

[Insert record scratch sound effect]

I said I am *not* going to start talking about guns! Sheesh.

Now, where was I? Oh, right. Extremes.

Our infatuation with them is prevalent in so many parts of our everyday lives. We intuitively know the pragmatic, healthy approach to getting through a normal day should include heavy doses of trying to work toward the center. There's perpetual talk about the need to achieve balance. However, in reality, we simply don't play in that sandbox very often. Because let's face it...moderation is no fun!

In our culture of pushing limits, we constantly hear people speaking in terms of absolutes. Something *always* happens. Something else *never* happens. They have *everything*. We have *nothing*. *Everybody* has this. *Nobody* has that. But in most cases, we know the truth ~~always~~ often falls somewhere in the middle. See? Those absolutes are so tempting!

With Disruptive Discovery, this magnetic attraction to the extremes is very useful. Identifying those outer margins, and the space between, helps us gain deeper levels of understanding with experiences and those involved. To achieve that function, we can employ another Question That Matters. This type of question is known as Range-finding.

Utilizing this approach, we create a platform for people to easily delve into their frames of reference so that the positive and negative ends of their experiential spectrums can be uncovered. Essentially, we want to see how they view "really good" and "really bad" through their own lenses.

By understanding their perceptions of this range, we take a few more strokes toward becoming a master artist helping people to paint a picture of the better place where they're hoping to arrive.

WHY DOES IT MATTER?

The responses to this genre of experiential-based inquiry are very revealing. We learn what people believe represents their boundary lines. These details serve as powerful reference points because expectations are formed in this manner.

That's right. Our expectations of today are heavily influenced by our experiences of yesterday, the day before yesterday, last year, all the scars—correction, blissful memories—from our childhood, and so on. Are you getting the drift? What happened in the past is instrumental in creating the borders around what we now expect.

There are opposite ends of this spectrum, the positive and the negative. On the positive side, we learn what people view as highly favorable. These could be outcomes they consider exceptional or environments that kindle strong connections to comfort. Conditions they would like to protect, keep, or repeat again.

On the other end, the negative extreme, descriptions of experiences less than stellar highlight what people would like to avoid or potentially change. These are the edges of perceived cliffs. Most people avoid such drop-off points, but not us. We are Disruptive Discoverers! I'll save you a Google search. Yes, it's really a word.

Like moths, we're attracted to those bright yellow caution signs. They clearly signal where the road ends, but they also represent where the discomfort starts. These insights are really helpful to know when rocking boats, and that's exactly what we do.

Another reason Range-finding questions matter is because they have an uncanny ability to expand Openings. A superhandy instrument as you assist others with either finding an enhanced solution for a problem or improving a development area. To over-refresh your memory, an Opening is the difference between Current and Aspirational States. It captures the variance between where someone *is* and the place they *want to be*. These questions can play a significant role in probing deeper into our understanding of the Opening that exists for the individuals or groups participating in this process.

They have exceptional value in taking our awareness of Aspirational States to new heights. Satisfying experiences lead to positive reinforcement. Knowing what outcomes people have found enjoyable or gratifying allows us to predict what they'd like to repeat and potentially eclipse.

This is an exercise in gaining a purposeful realization of the fringes and limits of those we're trying to help, enabling a clearer vision of their experiential reference points.

WHEN DOES IT MATTER?

Striking when the iron is hot would be advised with this type of question. As we discussed in Chapter 10, the process for moving beyond Surface Discovery involves offering a recap of the Opening, followed by a Transition question. If an encouraging response to this exchange transpires, we're presented with a perfect opportunity to move farther into Disruptive Discovery.

There are several mile-markers that represent the best time to push the accelerator, through the use of Range-finding questions as we travel down our Disruptive Discovery highway:

Conveying of expectations—Establishing beliefs around what participants expect to happen must take place early in the process. Making progress and achieving success within facilitation scenarios involves supposing certain outcomes and an anticipation of the resulting consequences. Without getting everyone involved on the same page with these forecasts, disappointment and frustration is highly predictable. With this sort of questioning, we have access to a vehicle that can allow for capturing and communicating these extremely important expectations.

Verifying the Opening—It's very common for an initial recap of the Opening to be mostly accurate, but not entirely complete. The assessment could potentially need more clarity and additional confirmation. We need to know whether the expressed Aspirational State closely matches the positive end of their experiential range. In other words, have experienced outcomes satisfied where they want to be or have they fallen short? On the other end, we need a check and balance in determining how the identified Current State looks compared to the negative extremes they've encountered or are trying to avoid. If they're close in proximity, this helps solidify awareness and perhaps increases motivation to make a change. If that negative end of the range is below the Current State, we've helped them realize they aren't experiencing such lows—at least, not yet. This will also reinforce what they want to avoid or protect against.

Assigning values—Once the threshold has been crossed and we have entered into Disruptive Discovery, the end result will depend greatly on how much we're able to learn about what is important to the players involved. Range-finding questions asked early and often become effective in getting a fix on what they value. I'm not necessarily speaking of values from a moral or ethical standpoint, but more related to their interests and priorities.

Stimulating conversation—A successful Opening recap and Transition question doesn't guarantee an outpouring of new information being shared. A natural pause sometimes takes place. If this momentum loss isn't the result of a change in the trust dynamic, sometimes additional effort, through stirring the dialogue, is needed to get people talking. These questions are a prudent method for tapping into different emotions, high and low, and can organically awaken the conversation. This helps to move things forward with our ever-present goal of deepening levels of under-standing in relevant areas across the board.

HOW *IS IT ASKED IN A WAY THAT MATTERS?*

Compared to "What if?" and "So what?" these questions are far less complex to ask. And I dare say they can lead to exchanges that are enjoyable for the Facilitator and everyone else involved. Range-finding is a time for rumina-tion. When sharing positive experiences, this is a seemingly congenial activ-ity. With negative experiences, it might sound contradictory, but sometimes recalling unpleasant events can also have a productive, forward-looking impact. Because we're asking people to share past occurrences, they can be viewed as somewhat nonthreatening. They're history, viewed in the rearview mirror, but could also be lessons learned to avoid in the future. In some cases, with the passage of time, a good laugh can be had because the benefit of perspective is firmly in place. I said in *some* cases.

But tread lightly. These could be instances that caused pain or dam-age. The potential for tearing down the walls of trust we've been building can more than offset the amount of understanding equity to be gained by poking at those sore spots.

So far, we have established the rationale for questions aimed at uncov-ering a spectrum of experiences and the different times in which they should be utilized. I then made a bold prediction by stating that the inter-action with this type of knowledge pursuit should be smooth and plea-surable, provided we can work around certain sensitivities. You might be wondering if there's a catch. There must be an advanced or convoluted way to properly ask these questions. Nothing is that easy, is it? This is fair skepticism, but my response is pretty underwhelming.

You ask by asking.

Sometimes we just don't need to overcomplicate things. Range-finding questions are straightforward. The only additional guidance I'll offer is that they tend to work most effectively when used in a comprehensive package, addressing both ends of the range. Perspective about positive experiences is often more evident when jointly considering those that were less than positive and the other way around. I offer this tidbit of wisdom based on a long history of trial and error with these inquiries.

Furthermore, starting on a high note, by initially concentrating on the superlatives, is usually the best way to commence the search for extremes. From there, the transition to not-so-fond remembrances is a more user-friendly exercise in comparison. I would relate this sequence to taking advantage of gravity by racing downhill versus fighting against it when plodding uphill. Take it from a guy who has run up and down his fair share of hills and go with the descending trail. Your legs will thank you.

WHAT *ARE SOME EXAMPLES OF IT MATTERING?*

We can take advantage of the natural flow that emerges with Range-finding questions when used in conjunction with one another. There are several tried-and-true packages that I have exuberantly put to use over the years. Each of them could be readily available for you to use as an entrée into learning about the span of experiences. Based on my own learning curve, I should inform you that there's a particular grouping that I've come to use most frequently. I refer to this go-to base pairing as Best/Worst. I realize this is probably self-explanatory, but, just to be safe, the positive extreme is addressed through questions utilizing "Best." The opposite, or negative limit, is tested by asking about happenings involving "Worst."

To illustrate how it works, think of a sales professional attempting to understand the needs of a potential customer. Continuing to reinforce starting with the more palatable question as the optimal bet, I recommend they ask,

What do you like best about the product you're currently using?

We should call attention to a key word in this example. By incorporating "like" as a specific term, the question taps into emotions, seeking to learn about feelings. Of course, the reverse, with an added sprinkle of setup, might look like:

I do realize it's not always pleasant to discuss such things, but please know that there's legitimate value in the question I am about to ask. If you had to pick something, what do you feel is the worst attribute of that product?

I have been accused of sometimes sounding like a broken record. I disagree. A broken record would uncontrollably remind you that the word choices in these questions are intended to stimulate emotion. But I'm not a broken record, so you can disregard that comment, unless I say it again.

There are certainly other variations at our disposal. A long list of different adjectives or adverbs can be substituted for Best/Worst, and I think it makes sense to highlight a few of them. Another iteration I find very effective is Most/Least. This combination has a slightly less polarizing tone. A business leader collaborating with their team on potential changes to a benefit in the company program could replace Best with Most in a Range-finding question and ask,

What characteristics of our benefits package, as it looks today, do our employees like the most?

At the other end of the spectrum, they could swap Worst with Least and inquire,

What do we think they like least about it?

Another combination that pushes the boundary lines is Favorite/ Unfavorite. It is, of course, similar to Best/Worst and Most/Least. However, you're more likely to get a very specific response with this one. People tend to reserve the crown of "favorite" for experiences residing at the tip-top of any list.

Depending on the nature of any grouping, corresponding emotional intensity could be elicited. To demonstrate this point, we can consider the pairing of Love/Hate. You would be hard-pressed to find words that evoke more emotion.

Surely there are plenty of other workable combinations. You can use flexibility and creativity while reading the room and adapt to the circumstances accordingly. But I believe we've covered the primary bases.

That wraps up our synopsis of Range-finding as a Question That Matters. A moment ago, as we were winding down the overview of different examples, I alluded to the use of creative juices. Do me a favor and hold that thought. It correlates nicely to the next chapter and should allow us to cruise on in. I'm talking about imagination, and it will be a central character in the upcoming tale.

Put on those warm jammies, say your prayers, make a wish, and get under the covers. It's bedtime and I have a story to tell.

15

QUESTION THAT MATTERS #4

DARE TO DREAM

R elax. I'm not really going to tell you a bedtime story. That would be weird, to say the least. You caught me in an embellishment, but some leeway would be nice. I was trying to set the tone and pique your interest in this chapter through foreshadowing with that off-the-mark reference. My roundabout thinking was that you go to bed, fall asleep, and then, of course, you dream. Are we good?

Hey, what can I say? Sometimes my cutesy attempts at being poetic work. But I'm fully aware those instances are the exception. Nonetheless, you don't need to worry. I'm undiscouraged and will keep swinging for the fences!

Back to our abstract concept…

For this Question That Matters, we aren't referring to dreams in the sense of those common, recurring nighttime delusions we all know so well. You know what I'm talking about. Those fantasies about falling, flying, being late, the test you're totally unprepared to take, or that horrifying feeling of your teeth falling out! Dissecting those dreams is between you and your therapist. In the context we'll be using in this discussion, dreams represent a visualization process. A way of encouraging people to use their right brains and get their heads in the clouds, imagining future possibilities.

But I would be remiss if I failed to mention the opposite kind of dream, better known as a nightmare. For the most part, I've found the type of question discussed in this chapter to be most effective when promoting a yearning for best possible outcomes and wishful thinking. However, value might also potentially exist in learning from doomsday or worst-case-scenario dreams.

Have you ever seen a movie or watched a cartoon or read a book in which someone finds a magic lantern, they rub it, and a genie pops out? Well, this is exactly like that except, unfortunately, I don't know where you can find a good magic lantern these days. And that means no genie, so I guess the fun has been sucked out of this analogy. Whatever. We can keep rolling with it. Dare to Dream questions allow people to think about their unique situation in an uninhibited way. If granted three wishes meant for getting them to a better place, what would they be?

WHY DOES IT MATTER?

As we've established, Range-finding questions are based on experiences. Dare to Dream questions go a few steps beyond and represent an exercise in visualizing, not limited by reality or actual events. They open doors to a nontraditional exploration of possibilities and lead to insights that result from stepping outside the oft-referenced box. By using this sort of question, we can learn what people value outside the recognizable known. We're handing them an instrument to express importance and priorities without any restrictions, limitations, or the shackles of their beliefs.

Notice the use of "beliefs" in that last sentence. What we believe is based on our confidence, convictions, or assumptions of perceived truths. But how do we know what's true? There's an age-old ideology that seeing is believing. When we see things, we experience them on some level. Once something has been experienced, we believe it. By connecting those dots, we see, we experience, we believe. Seeing is believing.

And therein lies the vicious cycle. Future outcomes are predicted based on past events. Round and round we go. The box people are always trying to think outside of starts to feel less like cardboard and more like one of those insanely frustrating escape rooms. How can something be possible if it hasn't actually happened? This could digress into a theological conversation, but as I've previously stated…wrong book. I'm not even beginning to go there! Instead, I submit that we open our minds and imagine. This grants us the ability to translate the power of dreaming from a fantasyland into real world applications.

Dare to Dream questions can shift an Aspirational State to a higher level. They can serve as an illumination for people in becoming aware of their better place that's different, enhanced, or more inspiring than previously considered. It can change the coordinates on their where-they-want-to-be map.

Asking individuals or groups to describe a best-case scenario is helpful in getting more detail on their Aspirational State because it offers insights into the outcomes people view as supremely positive. These answers reveal what someone views as a most coveted outcome, what they hope to see, or what they're striving to achieve. They reveal a representation of their desires or possibly even a wish list for that genie, if he ever shows up.

WHEN DOES IT MATTER?

Daring to dream is souped-up range-finding. There are times in which we want to determine whether an Aspirational State exceeds the extremes identified or the expectations expressed with our Range-finding questions. These different question types can often occur in sequence. Following Range-finding queries with Dare to Dream exercises creates a natural progression. An experiential-based extreme flows into a boundary-breaking contemplation of endless potentialities.

These questions are also exceptionally useful when trying to put the final brush strokes on our painting of the better place at which we're helping people to arrive. When the responses strengthen our understanding of an Aspirational State, that picture on the canvas becomes a masterpiece.

Nay, a Picasso! (On the subject of dreams, one of mine has been to find the perfect opportunity for using the word "nay." Another major accomplishment off my bucket list. Nice!)

It has been professed that if you don't like what people are saying, change the conversation. This can be necessary when others get stuck in their own paradigms, a somewhat debilitating condition resulting from the confining walls of past experiences, what they have been told, or some type of an "If it ain't broke, don't fix it" status quo mindset. The mental workout of wonderment may be set in motion at a time in which it's becoming apparent that expectations are unnecessarily low. Maybe they're settling for mediocrity or hesitant to step out of a comfort zone. Or their mind is closed because of failing to consider exhilarating prospects outside what they've known to be true. When people intellectually break through their glass ceilings, conversations can change because Aspirational States become a destination they hadn't previously visited. They transform into dream vacations at luxury resorts.

HOW *IS IT ASKED IN A WAY THAT MATTERS?*

When engaging in this activity, Facilitators are encouraging individuals or groups to describe desirous scenarios. To create that type of environment, we should call upon words and phrases that invoke thinking big or shooting for the stars. Words matter, and this is very true with Dare to Dream questions. I'll share some suggestions for specific words and positioning in just a minute.

Equally important are the unspoken words or nonverbal messages we incorporate in our activation of this question. I contend there are two main reasons for such a pronouncement. First, there might be a temptation for someone to dismiss your attempt to discover in this manner, or not take it seriously. They could interpret such a question as a frivolous exercise. Even though we're talking about using imagination and "dreaming," this is the furthest thing from playtime. Thoughtful responses can lead to compelling progress in the Disruptive Discovery process. Because of that potential impact, Dare to Dream questions deserve to be treated with a certain amount of gravity. Body language and nonverbal cues can nurture the rightful respect for this method of questioning. Genuinely employing eye contact, a look of interest, and listening skills as they start to share their thoughts are imperative.

Next, this type of question needs to be asked in an inviting manner. You're welcoming people to use their mental agility, and that can cause discomfort. It can potentially lead to feelings of vulnerability and insecurity. Smiling, head nodding, and engaging in other nonverbal communications will go a long way toward minimizing any feeling of insecurity. These can be fun, energizing, and invigorating questions to answer under the right circumstances.

The challenge becomes translating these expressed dreams into reality. After all, how do we mold thoughts into a practical form when they start as imaginative, visionary, or maybe even slightly whimsical? Better yet, to take large steps in the direction of being sensible, how do they become achievable or implementable? Several chapters ago, we discussed the role of Clarifying questions with Interactive Listening. It was a relatively brief mention but very much worth revisiting. The truth is that this ten-pack of Questions That Matter almost had an eleventh comrade. I gave a lot of thought and consideration to whether this highly serviceable, obscurity-clearer should be included in the list. Clarifying questions are major players, in general. They should be used early and often in both Surface Discovery and Disruptive Discovery. However, I ultimately decided that they thrive when used in conjunction with other Questions That Matter versus operating as a stand-alone entity with its own unique function. As a case in point, they often have a vital role to play with Dare to Dream questions in accurately deciphering what's being shared. These questions serve a few purposes:

- We must ensure that our understanding of what is being communicated matches the spirit of what is being imagined. Clarifying questions are useful in getting on the same page.

- They convert pie in the sky to the real world. Clarifying questions are convenient devices for the translation of fiction into nonfiction, abstract into concrete.

With that in mind, I'm guessing you could use a little more clarity right about now, and that's just what the doctor ordered.

WHAT *ARE SOME EXAMPLES OF IT MATTERING?*

If I had to pick one Question That Matters as the least self-explanatory, Dare to Dream probably takes the cake. As I have been speaking of enigmatic ways to conjure creativity, you might have been wondering, "How in the heck do I do that without other people thinking I'm nuts?" I'll say it again…words matter. They just do.

Specific examples of words and terms you can use when framing this type of question should aid in lifting the cloudiness. Check these out:

Dream (duh!)	**Ideal**	**Wish**	**Perfect**
Imagine	**Pretend**	**Optimal**	**Ultimate**
Fantasize	**Quintessential**	**Magic**	**Unlimited**
Assume	**Anything**	**Possibilities**	**Best-case**
Utopia	**Endless**	**Everything**	**Unconditional**

To go a step farther, I thought there would be value in assembling a collection of semiquestions that have potential application in many common personal and professional settings that might be encountered. What is a "semiquestion"? I don't know exactly. Just made it up. I'm really liking these poetic license privileges, and that sounded like a fitting description for this sampling, based on their incompleteness. Take a look and I think you'll get the gist.

A consultant working with a client might start a Dare to Dream question with:

In a perfect world, what would you expect…

A parent attempting to teach values to their child:

What if you could have anything and everything you want?*

A manager collaborating with one of their direct reports:

Tell me about your wish list for resources needed to...

A coach helping a player:

Pretend you have superpowers and could somehow use magic to...

A sales professional seeking to understand the aspirations of a customer:

Could you describe how you would spend an unlimited budget for...

An adviser supporting a friend who is struggling with a life decision:

Imagine for a moment that money was no object...

A community leader attempting to promote a new initiative:

Instead of focusing on the challenges involved, what is a best-case scenario that could happen...

The goal of sharing a few specific words, semiquestions, and applications was to make this question go from feeling understandably intimidating to much more palatable. Mission accomplished? I hope so.

There you have it. You are daring. You are a dreamer. You are now a Dare-to-Dreamer. We have invested a significant amount of time on this question. I've gone to great lengths with the aim of instilling a belief in

---

* I'm sure you recognize our old buddy "What if?" Dare to Dream questions often work nicely in that format.

its worth and almost begging you to espouse its value in the process of Disruptive Discovery.

But what if I did something really annoying? Like, I don't know, what would you think about me asking you to take a negative view or opposite perspective? Would you still be my friend if I challenged you to look away from the upside—now seen as clear as day—and to consider the downside of Dare to Dream questions? Would you be willing to muse over any damage that could be done by asking them?

Nah, I wouldn't do something so terrible or inconceivable. Would I?

16

QUESTION THAT MATTERS #5

THE OTHER SIDE

Contrarian \ku*h*n-trair-ee-*uh*n\ *noun* : a person who takes an opposing view, especially one who rejects the majority opinion.

have a confession to make. I'm helplessly one of these. But, in my defense, it should be noted that I'm not your run-of-the-mill contrarian. Many who claim this credential intentionally take the opposite position for the sport of it. They've adopted this identity as an excuse to hunt for conflict or entertain themselves. That isn't my modus operandi. Nope. I pride myself on being a well-intentioned contrarian.

There's that theme again…intentions.

I have a sincere desire to enhance outcomes, solve problems, assist development, and deepen relationships by challenging people to think differently and reconsider beliefs that are perhaps ripe for another examination. This Question That Matters is right up my alley. For any card-carrying contrarian, The Other Side is the place to be. It's where we enjoy spending time, hanging out, or chillin' with our peeps. However, those of us who possess such a natural inclination aren't part of a snooty, exclusive association. In fact, it's quite the contrary. If you are interested in asking this type of question, we're always accepting new members to our club and offer guest passes for those not ready to make long-term commitments. This is true because I know from experience that when you combine an authentic desire to help people with encouraging them to view a differing perspective, it can be a game-changing step toward cultivating Disruptive Discoveries.

I thought an anecdote would be a constructive way to get things kicked off with our dissection of this inquiry method...

Early in my career, I took the approach of keeping my eyes forward and focusing on whatever was in my line of sight. After several years, I got a wild hair, from being either antsy or bored, and decided to enroll in graduate school. I entered into a program to obtain my Master of Arts in Organization Development. Handling a full load of classes in addition to ambitiously driving my professional career packed with often overwhelming responsibilities, on top of a crazy travel schedule, was a downright grind.

Wah, wah. What a whiner. Yes, I get it. This was not some unprecedented, heroic undertaking. Everyone is busy, they work hard, and all lead hectic lives. Many folks also deal with the rigors of travel. And I realize that more than a handful of people have accomplished the feat of earning degrees while keeping up with their day jobs. I'm also pretty confident that the majority handled it much better than I did. So, forgive me for coming off sounding self-important, but don't forget my ongoing pursuit of finding ways to impress you.

Anyway, when it was time to start hunkering down on a thesis, an important step in that process was presenting a hypothesis for approval. At that time, I was a naïve student trying to stay in my lane and not cause any trouble so that I could get my degree and run with it. Keeping my eyes on the prize, I did what seemed to be exactly what you were supposed to do at this stage of the game. I picked a topic that was interesting to me, in general, and tried to dress up my theory-to-be-proven in hopes of it getting a rubber stamp.

At that time, I was somewhat obsessed with passive-aggressive behavior. It's still one of my favorite interpersonal dynamics, and I wanted to explore the role it played within organizations. Brimming with confidence, I offered a predictable hypothesis statement to my professor. More or less, I wanted my master's project to concentrate on the negative impact of passive-aggressive behavior in the workplace.

The response from this professor was unexpected but marvelously contrarian. He said, "Of course, there is a negative impact of passive-aggressive behavior in the workplace. You are stating the obvious. What about the opposite? What if we flipped that hypothesis on its head?"

When he posed this challenge, my eyes widened and I distinctly remember feeling a burst of energy. He was talking my language. He was asking the type of questions with which I have a symbiotic relationship. They exist somewhere in my DNA.

In other words, he wanted me to make a counterargument by setting out to prove that benefits or prosperity could materialize for companies and their employees due to the presence of passive-aggressive behavior. No way, right? Guess again. That investigation became the focus of my thesis, and I learned so much by taking a really close look at this reverse stance. Want to know the actual title? Sure, no problem—*Things Are Not Always As They Appear: The Positive Impacts of Passive-Aggressive Behavior on Organizational Effectiveness.*

Catchy. Doesn't it just roll right off the tongue?

In the end, I was so fortunate, and remain grateful to this day, to have this professor lay down a contrarian-based challenge intended for me to engage in such a mind-opening journey. I finished my thesis and proudly hold this master's degree, in case you were wondering. Impressed yet? But in the spirit of continued full disclosure, I didn't receive a praiseworthy grade on the project. I'm not telling you the grade, so don't bother asking. In my defense, I remember submitting my final project online in the wee hours of the morning during one of those sleepless nights a few weeks after my first Daughter was born.

To close the loop and bring us back to the outset, there's more involved with effectively asking The Other Side questions than trying to channel your inner contrarian. It's more about becoming a catalyst for people to think upside down or inside out by considering the antithesis.

WHY *DOES IT MATTER?*

I'm sure you've heard many different quotes and sayings speaking to the multifaceted nature of any situation. For example, it's been said that there are two sides to every story, and the truth is usually somewhere in the middle. And it's not difficult to find other citations out there referencing the ever-present reality of a third side, whether acknowledged or not.

Robert Evans, the famous film producer, was quoted as saying, "There are three sides to every story: your side, my side, and the truth. And no one is lying. Memories shared serve each differently."

Not sure it could be summed up any better than that.

I've ascertained the idea of only being able to gain a complete picture of any situation by viewing it from more than one vantage point to be an undeniable certainty in this world. Unfortunately, efforts toward embracing this philosophy or putting the necessary emphasis into feeding diversity of thought (promo for a future plea) appear to be eluding us as a society. As a result, any sense of urgency in finding the middle ground is becoming more and more scarce. Without seeing an opposite or differing perspective, getting to the middle doesn't represent a different place. There's no movement from the current position. You stay where you are and things look exactly the same.

This is one of the reasons compromise might one day yield to the same fate as dinosaurs or *Saved by the Bell: The College Years*...extinction. Needless to say, open minds are just a tiny bit important in any situation involving people and the relationships that exist among them. I'm not exaggerating by cautioning that there's real danger in anyone getting entrenched in their perspectives and their perspectives alone. In addition to the obvious downside of them looking like a know-it-all, they risk being exposed to the equally damaging ramifications of having blind spots.

In the universe of economics and finance, everyone is familiar with the concept of opportunity cost. It represents the potential gains not realized by picking one investment over another. It's the what-could-have-been, alternate reality that haunts anyone who invests their money and keeps them perpetually kicking themselves for making the wrong choice.

Well, there is also an opportunity cost involved in the universe of thinking. A closed mind means you could be missing out on potential benefits that could take place with other options. The only way we can minimize our opportunity costs is by stepping outside our own convictions. In addition, seeing only one side creates limitations, including stymieing creativity. These are known as blind spots.

But I need to highlight another important force at play. On a daily basis, we deal with so many widely accepted rules of the world. They're assumed as truisms and commonly regurgitated, for no other reason than that they represent what we have always heard or been told. For instance, I mentioned a specific law of life in Chapter 4 related to change. There's a common, deeply held belief that people don't like change. That's simply not true. It's just not. But people throw this "fact" around like Halloween candy. There's so much value in encouraging people to challenge conventional thinking, whether those thoughts originated from themselves or elsewhere.

It's healthy to tap a complacent paradigm on the shoulder every once in a while and say, "Hey, can I talk to your rambunctious twin brother for a minute?" And there's nothing wrong with letting the status quo know that it's in the hot seat and needs to stay relevant if it's planning to stick around.

WHEN *DOES IT MATTER?*

Closed-mindedness originates from a need for self-preservation. It's a way we protect ourselves from the murky, unchartered waters that exist in scary and unknown places. We typically try to avoid anything that threatens feelings of safety and security. I could get superdeep and profess that we purposely close our minds as a coping mechanism or they unconsciously get closed as a defense mechanism, but that could get pretty heavy. For this discussion, we can simply say that our brains tend to resist the idea of losing ideals we hold dear or having to face any consequences that might result from challenging our own beliefs. In short, holding on to our normal thinking is reassuring for our sometimes delicate psyche. And please forgive me for pulling you down the rabbit hole. I have more than a few strong feelings about the importance of these behavioral subtleties. Next, we simply need to add context to the way all this psychological mumbo jumbo relates to the right time for grabbing someone by the hand and leading them to The Other Side.

As Facilitators of the Disruptive Discovery process, we need to maintain a high level of awareness with other participating individuals around the mindsets just described. When you witness an expression of related feelings or emotions, responding accordingly with The Other Side questions can be both appropriate and effective. But in the absence of such a visible demonstration or emoting, how would we know they're bubbling under the surface? They often manifest through a few different warning signals:

- Thinking appears to be shut off, narrow, or constricted. People might ignore new ideas, pretending they didn't hear them. Or they placate others by pretending to consider their ideas when they're secretly trying to find the best way to squash them, often in a patronizing tone.

- A more severe manifestation occurs when there's a defensiveness, maybe even aggression, toward anything not supporting their own ideas, beliefs, or proposed solutions. Actions in this circumstance can look and feel like an attack against anything remotely contradictory.

Leaning toward safeguards also presents itself in group or team settings. Those behaviors might show in ways we've already covered. But, unfortunately, there is another phenomenon that can quickly and easily happen at the drop of a dime. These environments often foster conditions leading to groupthink. The bad news is that groupthink breeds conformity. And if conformity is oil, freethinking is water. The good news is that engaging a cadre of people in the exercise of considering alternative perspectives can help break the commonly irresistible force of groupthink.

We are all guilty of sticking to our guns or displaying signs of stubbornness. I've seen piles of money evaporate into the thin air of casinos when headstrong gamblers refuse to bet on red after it hits for the umpteenth time. Or, in a simple game of coin flipping, we keep calling "heads" and won't entertain the idea that "tails" is equally possible. But make no mistake…helping people realize there's a different picture on the other side of the coin is so important in their ability to gain invaluable perspective.

HOW *IS IT ASKED IN A WAY THAT MATTERS?*

This Question that Matters is one that requires posing in a deliberate manner. With anything disruptive, shaking the foundation can be incredibly rewarding. But fruitful shakes can become a catastrophic, 7.9 on the Richter scale earthquake, if not managed properly. I recommend following these guidelines to avoid your facilitations being reduced to rubble:

- ✔ First, check your intentions. You are NOT looking for an argument or picking a fight. This is about trying to help people get to a better place.

- ✔ Next, this is a perfect opportunity to dust off the Empathator (that's a made-up name for an empathy machine and admittedly not my best effort). Encouraging an empathic mindset, for you and other participants, can be impactful with whetting appetites for stakeholders to see The Other Side. This allows people to walk in the shoes of someone else or see situations through a lens other than their own.

- ✔ Finally, we can't lose sight of the inherent challenge with a necessary component for considering an opposing point of view. Overcoming this barrier requires believing that a different perspective is needed or would add value. For that realization to happen, an ample supply of self-awareness must be present. People need to be aware that their views are THEIR views and not the views of all mankind. Other perspectives do exist, whether they want to accept that or not. This doesn't happen without self-awareness. I would even recommend a helping of self-deprecation for those who are capable. Remember, our role in this process is that of a Facilitator. By definition, self-awareness happens within one's self. It can't be given, sold, or lent. But we can certainly look for opportunities to outwardly promote how being cognizant of ourselves is pretty darn special.

Remember, our goal is to ask a question that invites people to do a headstand with their views. We want to rock paradigms and force archetypes out of their comfy recliners stuffed with potentially stifling blind spots.

WHAT *ARE SOME EXAMPLES OF IT MATTERING?*

Have you ever dealt with someone who is adamant in their position or insistent their view is the right one? Yes, that was a rhetorical question. Maybe it's a friend or a family member. Maybe it's a boss, an associate, or a client. Or maybe it's the inflexible posturing of a customer service representative causing your temper to teeter on detonation. In any of those situations, you could try working overtime to win an argument and change their mind. Good luck with that. Some people love disagreements and don't miss an opportunity for a good debate. So, serve one on a platter. But instead of wrangling with *you*, turn the tables and encourage them to argue with *themselves*. This alternate outlet would lead to otherwise unlikely progress:

> *You have been strongly pushing for this option and I'm curious about something. How would you argue against it?*

There are many different styles and variations that could be used to ask this question. Use your best judgment and defer to your room-reading acumen. The goal is raising awareness of a differing perspective and getting another individual, or group, to take a peek at it. Here are a few other potential interpretations of how The Other Side questions could look in practice:

We have a strong understanding of our value proposition and the ways we are better than the competition. If* they were in a similar meeting talking about our company, what would they say?

The benefits of that decision are very clear, assuming things work as planned. If some unexpected twists take place, should we anticipate any disadvantageous outcomes?

Well, it's very clear that you aren't seeing eye to eye with her. Even though she shares a different view, is there any area in which you agree?

That was an interesting comment. How do you think what you just said would resonate with your teammates?

And let's think about another scenario I'm sure sounds familiar…
Someone excitedly floats an idea to the group. Just as momentum and energy start to build, a dissenting voice says with a smirk, "Oh, we tried that in the past and it didn't work." That's a zinger that can wickedly deflate a once-promising solution. Previously breathable air is typically replaced with one of the following types of gases:

- Defensive clinging to positions = bad feelings
- Silent dismissal of the idea = resentment

Fear not, there's another option. What about asking a The Other Side question? Oxygen can be salvaged in the room by trying:

---

* Hey there, "What if?" It's you again!

I'm assuming there was a great reason you originally tried it in the first place. What was the rationale?

Or

I'm wondering if there were any positive results from that last attempt. Is it possible the problem occurred in its execution and not the idea itself?

Lastly, because we've talked extensively about the dangers and limitations of keeping our minds closed and only seeing one side, we should put this Question That Matters to the test. I have a few mind-benders that could use your mulling over:

- What are the advantages of a closed mind?
- Is there any benefit in seeing only one side of a situation?

Based on everything we just covered, those sound like ridiculous questions, right? Nobody would blame us for conveniently dismissing them as nonsense. That would be a reasonable and intelligent thing to do. And it would also represent one of the sins that I try to avoid at all costs. Hypocrisy.

Let's not fall into that trap. Take a moment and think about those questions. I'll bet you can fight through the awkwardness and discomfort. It might feel a little naughty, but I'm guessing you might learn a thing or two in the process.

Liberating, isn't it?

17

QUESTION THAT MATTERS #6

IMPETUS

Why do you get out of bed in the morning?

No, that's not a Question That Matters, but it's a doozy. And I'm not being facetious. I staunchly believe everyone should contemplate what's behind their daily routines and packed calendars. We should look beyond our to-do lists by giving the deserved amount of reflection to the wherefores of rising and shining. The answers don't tell us everything we need to know about people, but they come pretty darn close.

I want to take that angle a step further. After crawling out from under those snuggly covers and dragging our sleepy eyes to the source of whatever caffeine fix we crave, there's a question that follows us all day, every day.

Why do we do *anything*?

The answer is so simple and yet so complicated. The reason people do anything—and I do mean anything—is due to the presence of motivation. It's the spirit and energy that induces behavior. There are always stimuli leading to actions. We just need to pinpoint them and supply the necessary nourishment to thrive.

Before going any further, we should probably talk about that power word for a minute. We have referenced this condition of the mind quite a bit since throwing in together.

Motivation.

It emerged as a prevalent theme when covering *our* intentions, fit, and purpose in the Disruptive Discovery process. However, equally, if not more importantly, is the motivation of other people participating in our facilitation. Certainly the amount of motivation involved is a factor, but what we really want to know is its origin. Put another way, what's specifically motivating, or hindering, *them* to change behaviors and actions as a route to find better solutions for challenging problems or to improve in a particular development area? And, with that, we are only looking at the tip of the iceberg...

What we often don't see underwater, as part of those giant floating ice cubes, are motives. I'm not trying to confound you with a play on words here. Motives are a precondition to motivation. There's an important distinction between those closely related terms. If motivation is *how* behaviors and actions come to fruition, motives are the reasons behind them. In layman's terms, motives represent *why* anyone would want to behave or act in the first place. Before there is inclination (motivation) there must be purpose (motives).

From a Disruptive Discovery standpoint, our mission is to gain insight into what carries people from their motives to motivation. The bridge over that gap is known as an impetus. And the vehicle we'll use to understand how others translate an initial sense of purpose into action are Impetus questions.

Sometimes this driving force is conscious or even calculated. But in other instances, the energy could be building at a subconscious level. Regardless, getting our arms around the root cause will ultimately pay handsome dividends as we help people get to where they're trying to go.

Before we delve into our favorite WHY, WHEN, HOW, and WHAT workout routines, I should mention a different question always lurking in the background when human beings interact with other human beings, either on an individual basis or in group settings. And it's typically used as an acronym we know very well...

WIIFM

I do find it humorous that this acronym is so commonly spoken with a straight face. What a strange-sounding word. We pronounce it like "wiffum." That just has a funny ring to me. Wiffum. But I guess it saves us, like, three syllables versus forcing ourselves to enunciate all those terribly burdensome words. Our laziness never ceases to amaze me.

What's In It For Me?

There it is. Good ol' WIIFM. The answer to this question is what our species perpetually wants to know. And its askers aren't limited to any particular demographic. People of all ages, ethnicities, genders, nationalities, and religious affiliations welcome this beloved friend with open arms. I don't think WIIFM has ever been a victim of any discrimination, and it gets plenty of equal opportunities across all questioners.

This acronym is a simple, convenient means for us to condense our obsession with self-interest into five awkwardly combined letters, three consonants and two side by side vowels. Rest assured that anyone involved in your facilitation of Disruptive Discovery is asking themselves this question. There's no two ways about it.

As individuals seek their own answers to this question, their responses fall along another spectrum. It might seem that ranges are another recurring theme and perhaps more common than you previously realized. For this continuum, the gamut of WIIFM goes from altruism to egoism.

With altruism, people find their primary value through the act of caring for others. A selfless act would represent a purist form of altruism. Although, if you remember, earlier I challenged their attainability at all. It's quite possible this is another cynical hang-up on my long list, but I'm not buying the idea of any act being completely devoid of benefit for the person performing said act. That's my story and I'm running with it. Regardless, there's no denying that altruism is very real, and finding fulfillment through offering support to folks within your circles is an admirable value to possess.

On the other end of the WIIFM spectrum is egoism. Here, the individual asking this internal question would unashamedly wish all benefits of their interactions with others to center on themselves, an obvious form of selfishness. But wanting to know what you get for what you give goes beyond the transactional nature of the literal question itself. There is a direct link to the motivations that lead to behaviors and actions.

How do we discover the impetus responsible for carrying or pushing each individual involved in the process to their all-important motivations? It's not an easy task. Fortunately, you came to the right place. I'll do my best to lend a hand…in a selfless way, of course.

WHY *DOES IT MATTER?*

Sometimes the best strategy is to lead with a statement and then back it up with supporting details. Unfortunately, as you're becoming more and more aware, I'm chronically guilty of the reverse approach. As I try to rein in my compulsion, here's a best-foot-forward attempt at a WHY proclamation for this Question That Matters: *Impetus questions are used to uncover the driving forces of motivation so that we can understand how to help others move toward action.*

Kabam! Killed it! And now comes the hard part of laying down the backup.

Impetus questions unveil the motives that are bottled up within people. Once we're able to gain a clear vision of what will drive them to act, it becomes much easier for us to conceptualize the most appropriate game plan to be used with an individual or group in the Disruptive Discovery process. If momentum can be generated with this knowledge, it can carry all the way to motivation. So, we should take the learnings from these questions and reconstruct them into the propulsion that can take everyone to the better place they're trying to reach.

Again, there's a driving force connected to motivations. Impetus questions serve as a resource to reveal them. As I have interacted with individuals and groups over time, it's been a pleasure to make the acquaintance of an array of motivations. Based on these experiences and observations, I have compiled a list of the most-often encountered motivations and organized them into pairings (each representing its own scale between opposite points). Here are those duos, along with brief descriptions:

- *Essential*–Completely necessary, even crucial to survival
- *Nonessential*–Related to growth and development

- *Internal*–Your own conscious decision to do something for yourself or other people
- *External*–Influenced by stimuli from outside environments or circumstances

- *Discretionary*–On your own proactive terms
- *Pressing*–Reactive response to requests or obligations, possibly mandatory

- *Explicit*–Others are aware
- *Passive*–Others aren't aware

- *Altruistic*–Benefits derived from helping others
- *Egoism*–Focused on serving your own needs

As you witness any indicators of motivation during your direct collaboration efforts or indirect surveillance, attempt to diagnose the specific types. If they can be properly labeled, you're in business. This comprehension offers clarity in the hand you've been dealt. Armed with such understanding, you can plug away at the factors that ultimately lead to behaviors and activity. They also assist with an ability to gauge levels of determination and commitment.

Moreover, we can learn about the origins or causes of motives at play. Knowing the source of energy fueling any of these motivations is powerful, to say the least. With this alertness, we can work on harnessing it, building on it, and pointing it in the right direction.

WHEN DOES IT MATTER?

You could argue that the answer is simple, possibly even laughably so. When do Impetus questions matter?

Always.

And that's true because—cliché analogy time—motivation is like the wind for a sailboat. With lots of it, those billowed sails will take you just about anywhere. Without it, you might as well crack open a few cold ones and enjoy the scenery because your oomphless vessel ain't going anywhere.

But that would be the easy answer. I don't particularly care for easy answers. Plus, there's a better explanation. In the Disruptive Discovery process, there are two opportune occasions likely to present themselves in which this question matters the most: in the early stages and when momentum shifts.

First, Impetus questions are instrumental at the beginning of the process because they can help us chart a course or create a Disruptive Discovery plan that would be most effective. These inquiries should kick off once purpose has been established and there's initial movement within Surface Discovery.

Second, this Question That Matters is timely at any point during the process, when you sense a different energy or a changing of the tides. This could present itself as modified behaviors, inconsistent activity levels, or any other new dynamics you detect. You might also sense a reversal, an adjustment, or a shifting momentum with an identifiable driving force. Understanding the nature of evolving impetus can be telling in many ways.

HOW *IS IT ASKED IN A WAY THAT MATTERS?*

In this case, there is, in fact, a very uncluttered answer. These questions must be asked using one of my favorite qualities.

Authenticity.

To be more specific, a genuine curiosity can go a long way toward getting the most bang for your buck with Impetus questions. Otherwise, they can sound like one of those vacuous, canned interview probes like, "What are your greatest strengths?" or "Where do you see yourself in five years?"

There's a possibility that this type of questioning can be construed as touchy-feely, so the appropriate handling is necessary. Ask purposefully.

Listen intently. Learn vigorously. Be in the moment. In a nutshell, being authentic wins the day with this Question That Matters.

WHAT ARE SOME EXAMPLES OF IT MATTERING?

I could be lazy and sidestep my responsibilities by referring back to the summary of motivations previously provided. Relevant questions can be crafted to discover the impetus involved in any scenarios fitting those descriptions. But we'll put in the hard work together because I can't have you losing respect for me.

Initiating dialogue bringing front and center what will push motives into motivation is our objective. I tend to latch on to concepts more fluently through tactile examples. My hunch is that I'm not alone, so maybe these mock-ups will make all this seem more practicable. By design, they give a touch of flavor to the means in which we invite others into understanding their bridge to motivation. And I'm staying with the hot hand by using fill in the blanks so these questions can be used in a wide range of personal and professional scenarios:

> *How would you define success with _____?*
> *What makes you happiest in your _____?*
> *In what ways do you directly benefit from _____? Any indirect benefits?*
> *Who else would benefit directly from _____? And indirectly?*
> *If _____ doesn't happen, what would you expect to occur?*
> *Is anyone else aware that _____ is important to you?*
> *The timeline of _____ was established by who or what?*
> *Can you share the ways in which you are measured with _____?*
> *How do you earn incentives or increased compensation with the _____ program?*

It's worth noting that none of these examples actually use the word "motivation." Yes, you could certainly flat-out ask what's motivating someone in any given situation. But their response could have debatable value for a few reasons. Frankly, that type of question is somewhat leading. It assumes that motivation exists in the first place, and that could be a flawed assumption. In addition, it can lead to the temptation of someone saying what they think sounds good or what they believe you want to hear. Either response does us no favors. Once again, we need feedback that speaks directly to what's behind any drive that's influencing behavior and action.

If you thought I was done talking about WIIFM, have we met? This self-interest query can be used in an advantageous way. You can seize the momentum of preexisting agendas. We can capitalize on the elephant in the room by acknowledging that everyone involved in any given situation must have their interests addressed and accommodated.

You see, WIIFM is a one-sided approach to any scenario. But by making this a multilayered exercise, and changing only a single letter in the acronym, you can engage and energize all stakeholders involved in the process. What exactly am I saying? Check out these variations and their fit with the corresponding mindsets:

WIIF__M__
What's In It For *Me?*
Internal mindset, and I'm pretty sure we've already covered this one.

WIIF__Y__
What's In It For *You?*
External mindset prioritizing the interests of others.

WIIF__U__
What's In It For *Us?*
Mutual Concern mindset. Now we're getting somewhere.

Three similarly clumsy sounding acronyms that couldn't be asking more dissimilar questions. As a Facilitator of Disruptive Discovery, the challenge is to get anyone participating with you honestly exploring all the above. They need transparency about the potential gains for themselves

(Me), everyone else (You), and the combination of both (Us). The answers will point directly to the impetus of the behavior or outcomes they're hoping to achieve.

I reckon you want to know if any of these WIIF versions stand above the rest as an Impetus question. You want me to say it, don't you? You want me to drop this neutral stance routine and pick a side. Because I don't want to be a killjoy and ruin the surprise, how about an itsy-bitsy teaser instead? Let's just say we might be preoccupied with the wrong acronym in our day-to-day. But no matter how much you beg, I'm not spilling the beans on which WIIF brings about the most mot-U-vation for getting us out of bed.

18

QUESTION THAT MATTERS #7

NARRATIVE

've always appreciated the skill involved with telling stories and admired those who've developed dexterity in captivating an audience with a tale. I do believe it's a gift…and apparently not a talent I have in my bag, according to my Wife and Daughters.

Here's a multiple-choice question for you:

When Geoff tells a story at home, he gets interrupted or his family loses interest:

A.) Never—They love all his stories and would never do such a thing.
B.) Rarely—But only if it's an emergency.
C.) Occasionally—And they feel terrible when it happens.
D.) *Every…single…time.*

I can't endure the humiliation of telling you the answer. Instead, I'll just say that either A, B, or C would be incorrect.

Now that I think about it, I honestly can't remember the last time I was able to complete a full sentence around that crowd. They lovingly tell me the problem is my cadence, and that I "talk too slow." But don't be fooled…that's what interrupters always say. Yeah, they blame the victim?!?! Just like bossy people blame their innocent prey with, "Well, if you knew what to do, I wouldn't need to tell you!"

I apologize for the unprompted tirade. Open wound. But I'm OK now. What was I saying? Ah, yes. I remember…

Storytelling.

This art of telling stories is most often used as a form of entertainment in social or cultural settings. However, it can also serve as an alternative means of discovering information versus a more traditional question-answering model. In this context, stories communicate thoughts, opinions, facts, and other details relevant to a situation or an idea being explored.

When observing people in these settings, I've noticed that a subtle yet substantial transformation emerges as they recount past events or speculate about the future. An unleashing of the extrovert within sometimes takes place. In some cases, this is a natural extension of their personality. However, there are other instances in which relatively mellow individuals who are otherwise reluctant to say much of anything absolutely light up when put in this position.

This could be due to intuitively knowing that storytelling taps into the emotions of the listeners. As a result, the information they're sharing becomes more persuasive, compelling, perhaps even inspiring. Or maybe they just enjoy spinning a tale. I'm not exactly sure, but either way, when gums start flapping, it creates opportunities for us to listen and learn.

This is all well and good, but some connecting of the dots between storytelling and Disruptive Discovery would assist in describing how they work together. Or, more specifically, the way telling tales meshes with a type of question that makes a difference.

Stories can be narrated. The act of narration is performed by sharing relevant experiences, giving examples, or describing an account of events in a storylike fashion. As mentioned, many people feel a level of ease in expressing themselves in this manner. The use of first, second, or third person voices seems either to boost confidence or create a sense of comfort or both.

We can stoke the fires for this form of expression by asking Narrative questions. This Question That Matters represents another option, a shiny new tool in the box, to gain insights and perspectives when the use of conventional queries requiring more straightforward responses might not be the ideal path to follow. Maybe this question is analogous to a newfangled plunger? You'll see where I'm going....

WHY *DOES IT MATTER?*

If telepathy was a real thing, there wouldn't be much need for this Question That Matters. Or, if you had psychic powers, we could skip it completely. For that matter, I guess you wouldn't need to ask *any* questions. Plus, that would be way cool, and I would really want to become your BFF.

Wait, *do* you have psychic abilities? Did you already know I was going to say what I just said?

Anyhow, it would be difficult to disagree with the notion of a talking dearth putting a mild strain on our ability to listen. As a result of this undeniable talk-listen phenomenon, these questions do, in fact, matter. The bottom line is that Narrative questions can represent effective icebreakers to get words flowing. Once that happens, as Facilitators, it becomes much more feasible for us to turn those words into information into knowledge into meaningful insights. Another way to view Narrative questions is by using them to "unclog" obstructions that participants might be battling.

Tool...plunger...unclog...I'm a downright poet laureate, huh?

These verbal barriers or blockages do present themselves and they aren't exactly rare. People frequently struggle when asked to respond to challenging questions, explain their ideas in an understandable way, or think in unfamiliar terms, both abstract and concrete. It's also worth noting that, even absent any hindrances, the sharing of anecdotes and experiences through narration in and of itself is filled with value. This form of expression allows for the promise of passing along learnings that are unique in quality. Those nuggets can be very revealing. People might even share details that would have otherwise been missed purely because this mode is more conducive to free-flowing information.

Another important reason to ask questions that encourage the portraying of relatable stories is because they open doors for citing real examples. This can often help people articulate what they're trying to say if encountering figurative stumbling blocks or hurdles in their communication efforts. They can either single out direct reference points or they can offer a more indirect illustration, as an interpretation of what they're attempting to get across. These narratives can help the storyteller spell out otherwise ambiguous details for both themselves and all listeners in an understandable way.

WHEN *DOES IT MATTER?*

Prolific volumes of research have been performed about sundry communication styles. A quick Internet search will show innumerable results on the subject. There are entire training courses and books dedicated to the various methods of understanding your style, properly identifying the styles of other people, and tactics for adjusting your style based on their style to create the perfect style. Typically, these techniques break down the different communication profiles into four categories or quadrants. There are even models containing a fifth style, as an added bonus, I presume.

My lighthearted tone isn't meant to poke fun at these models or dismiss the research that's been conducted. I have found these systems and concepts to be legitimate and then some. If I'm being honest, they're proven in practice as valid, credible, and often eerily accurate resources. I've even taught snippets here and there during some of my coaching and training activities.

But I just can't help myself. Allow me to lower my voice and tell you a secret. I should warn you that this is highly classified intelligence and leaking it to you won't make me popular in the training or consulting communities. Giving you this peek behind the curtain might land me smack-dab on one of those Wanted posters, but I like to live dangerously. Behold this shocking revelation…

Understanding communication styles isn't that complicated. It just isn't.

I don't think you need a novel or multiday training program dedicated to this topic. A much simpler, borderline common sense approach will do just fine. If you have less than sixty seconds to spare, I can try teaching you a vastly simplified technique. Communication styles can be determined by looking at two attributes for any individual:

Attribute #1—The amount of boldness, directness, and assertiveness they demonstrate.

Attribute #2—The amount of emotions and feelings they tend to display.

You simply assign a More or Less to each of those factors and, by grouping them into distinct combinations, some quick math gives you four different profiles. Voilà. That's basically the nutshell version. Call it Communication Styles 101. The last few paragraphs will self-destruct in…

For Narrative questions, I believe they're most effective when interacting with individuals exhibiting emotions and feelings on the More side of the scale, with Attribute#2. Some of these folks relish the process of describing details and warm up to the idea conveying their experiences in this manner. And others in this category view narration opportunities as a tool for relationship building.

I hope you don't misunderstand my point. If so, that's on me. To clarify, getting people with any communication style talking can lead to fantastic exchanges of information. I'm merely suggesting those who relate to emotions and feelings are more likely to associate with delivering their message through stories.

When one or more of the participants involved in your Disruptive Discovery process fits the profile, I'd recommend keeping this great option in your back pocket. If the question answering format being deployed is yielding limited responses, or you're witnessing closed nonverbal communication, it might be time to consider asking this Question That Matters as a next step. Just make sure you have previously confirmed their willingness to share information through a Transition question. With that arrangement firmly in place, feel confident to encourage them toward assuming a narrator role in the ongoing dialogue. This outlet should inject a feeling of comfort.

Another timely application of Narrative questions happens in scenarios relating directly to articulation abilities, or a deficiency with these abilities. I'm permitted to throw stones because I'm a member of the

Articulation Deficiency Society. This is one of my many flaws. Certainly, a less self-deprecating description would be referring to this problem as a quirk, or a nuance, of my character. But, alas, you earn the right to call it an undeniable flaw when your mouth routinely stumbles to stay on pace with your brain. I find myself constantly tangling with this challenge.

Specifically, I'm referring to situations when someone is struggling to verbalize an answer that's impalpable in their mind. This could be a mental scramble to put the puzzle pieces together. Or multiple replies to the same question are rattling around between the ears. Or the answer is crystal clear, but finding the right words to make it sound intelligible, even coherent, is exhaustingly frustrating for them.

This discourse might pass for a quasitherapy session because that last paragraph gave me some relief by chronicling the torture I face every day when trying to convey seemingly simple responses.

Can we agree that when situations arise in which someone is showing stymied expression efforts, they might appreciate the latitude of fleshing out their ideas through the telling of stories or reminiscences? On behalf of the many people who deal with these challenges, I'll say that fitting moments exist when Narrative questions make it easier for us. The right question at the right time lets us off the hook, so to speak. So, don't hesitate to ask them. It would be much appreciated, I assure you.

HOW *IS IT ASKED IN A WAY THAT MATTERS?*

Once upon a time, we talked about storytelling being a gift. For some, it's verbal craftsmanship, as displayed by my fairy-tale opening with that last sentence—ba-dum-bump. There's so much skill involved in knowing which details are important enough to include and where to place the necessary emphasis. As Facilitators, we aren't afforded the luxury of getting a giant tub of popcorn, sitting back, and enjoying the show. In fact, our role is contrary to that of a casual observer.

We have the responsibility of creating an atmosphere that allows the freedom and flexibility called for with this form of expression. A stage must be constructed using security, open-mindedness, and encouragement as props. Also, there's hard work, the heavy lifting we must undertake as interactive listeners. Staying engaged, both verbally and nonverbally, is critical to foster the necessary environment. Remember, this Question That Matters is a channel to gain information, thoughts, ideas, and insights. We're simply using storytelling as an alternative to traditional questioning. As participants are sharing or expressing themselves, we need to listen for those consequential details, the gems answering the questions that needed asking, even in this indirect manner.

If proper diligence is performed in these steps, we're setting up narrators for success. They can recall a relevant event that took place in the past, recite an anecdote that speaks to the topic at hand, or ponder what might happen if an idea becomes reality. Just get the stage ready and let them shine.

WHAT *ARE SOME EXAMPLES OF IT MATTERING?*

I know I've been blathering about asking people to tell stories in a way that might call up an image of making s'mores while hanging around a campfire. As much fun as that sounds, it obviously doesn't represent the type of Disruptive Discovery setting you're planning to promote. It's time now for us to look at Narrative questions through a practical lens and talk about specific ways they can be applied. And don't be surprised, or disappointed, with there being no mention of the words "story" or "tale" in these sample questions that could be used in the real world.

Here's the lowest hanging fruit representation of a Narrative question:

I'm so curious to hear your thoughts on _____ if you're open to sharing them?

Or some fruit on the next highest branch, but still fairly easy to reach:

Can you offer an example of _____?

And now fruit low enough that you don't need a step stool, but going on tiptoe might be necessary:

Would you mind giving more detail about _____?

Asking someone to teach you is a fantastic way to open the learning gates, while also helping them to either vet or reinforce what they already know:

Let's assume I know absolutely nothing about _____, would you explain it to me in a way that I'm able to comprehend?

Prompting recollection of past events that have commonality with a problem or development area can be done with this basic template:

Think about any similar situation you've encountered. If you have one in mind, could you share how it played out, including what worked or fell short?

Of course, the perfect follow-up Narrative question would be:

What would you do differently in the future?

Range-finding questions can also pull double duty as Narrative questions:

Could you tell me all about your favorite _____?
I think we could all learn a few lessons by hearing about the worst _____. It would be so helpful, and we were wondering if you would be willing to review what happened.

Putting someone in an impromptu brainstorming position can get the ball rolling:

When thinking about _____, describe what runs through your mind?

The questions themselves have a relatively low degree of difficulty. Beyond identifying the proper fit and timing, your mission is to sift through the voluminous flow of information using a listening skill sieve to capture the prizes that will move the process forward.

Speaking of s'mores, did you know they were invented in the 1920s? Originally, they were known as a graham cracker sandwich. Thankfully, the Girl Scouts published a recipe for s'mores in 1927 and gave us an all-time, can't-help-but-smile-when-you-say-it food name. You can thank me later for this bit of trivia (and it's a freebie). But enjoying the decadence of s'mores comes at a price. You endure gluey residue on your fingers, the very real possibility of a melted, chocolatey marshmallow blob on your lap, and the after-s'mores regrets of eating one too many, maybe a few more than one too many. In the end, we're forced to look ourselves in the mirror and honestly assess whether the indulgence was worth it....

Did the joy of such ecstasy outweigh the likelihood of s'mores-related fallout?

Sounds like a question that might just matter.

19

QUESTION THAT MATTERS #8

RISK/REWARD

At any given moment, I have lots of craziness swirling around in my mind. I'm not referring to the loose screw variety of crazy. Although, without a doubt, there's plenty of that run-of-the-mill crazy partying it up in there too. But right now I'm referring to craziness in the form of conversations, mostly arguments, I have with myself. Also, lots of fruitless ideas are likely brewing, with the occasional brain drizzle (not a storm) carrying a glimmer of hope for getting picked to make the team. And then, of course, there are countless thoughts my built-in filter thankfully never allows to see the light of day because, otherwise, I'd be living a lonely existence. Those are just a few of the performances taking place in the three-ring squirrel circus you can find inside my old bean. But there's also another type of activity going on in that crowded space throughout the day, as I deliberate various options and courses of action.

My mind is constantly calculating risk versus reward. A number-crunching routine involving the evaluation of potential benefits of any decision and comparing them to the possible liabilities. Some of this figuring is easy enough and needs nothing more than fingers and toes. Other judgments require an iPhone calculator app, or perhaps an abacus. On that note, did people actually ever use the abacus? Those gadgets look ridiculous, and I just can't imagine kids banging out their math home-work or adults doing their tax returns using one of them during ancient times. They take a lot of perhaps unwarranted shrapnel whenever I mock clinging to old ways of doing things and resisting the progressiveness of technology and innovation. I should probably either learn how to use one or find a new punching bag. There goes another digression. At this point my apologies are probably falling flat, so just know I'm working on it.

Continuing to overblow these computations, some assessments evaluating the ratio of risk to reward are so intricate and mind-boggling, it seems I need something to assist my overmatched frontal lobes. Maybe a microprocessor could be installed to cipher risk and reward data. Or I could program one of those stalkerlike algorithms used by websites that know exactly when to jump out of the online bushes with an advertisement for the new running shoes I just decided to think about buying a few hours earlier. How do they do that?

In all seriousness, this calculation is meant to switch a decision from subjective to objective. It's an attempt to provide clarity about a question people constantly grapple with answering. And it should be mentioned that this is a question we're all guilty of answering incorrectly.

Is it worth it?

As in, is the potential reward of what could be gained by doing something greater than the potential risk of what could be lost? It's imperative that I make something very clear: Substitution of "is" with "was" doesn't fly for this evaluation exercise. Doing so would make for a colossally disparate conclusion.

By asking "*Was* it worth it?" we have the benefit of hindsight. We'd be looking at situations in the past tense. They've already played out. In the business world, this is a component of the postmortem process, when it's used to identify lessons learned from the outcomes of decisions and projects. In our personal lives, we often spend hours living in the past, conversing with family and friends about whether a choice was good, bad, right, or wrong.

By inquiring "*Is* it worth it?" about some decision, we're looking into the future, playing out possible scenarios and determining whether the upside outweighs the down. We aren't attempting to predict the future.

Other Questions That Matter are used for that purpose. We're merely trying to project whether a speculation is attractive enough to roll the dice in the first place.

If you are wondering about the fit with Disruptive Discovery, I'll get right to the point. As participants in the process envisage various choices, decisions, options, or courses of action, this estimation can serve as a guide in selecting the best path. Facilitators like us can assist people as they perform these necessary assessments, evaluations, determinations, or whatever we want to call them, through the use of Risk/Reward questions. If any help is needed with addition or subtraction, we will be right by their side counting out loud. And now a word from our favorite four partners in crime.

WHY DOES IT MATTER?

We have many cognitive biases. If you're not familiar with these thinking patterns, I strongly suggest doing another quick Internet search (sorry, last time…maybe). It might just blow your mind, pun absolutely intended. A cognitive bias is a preconceived notion based on our experiences, perceptions, and what we think we know. Needless to say, they have a powerful influence on our decision-making and judgment. Depending on the specific research source, the number of cognitive biases is somewhere in the neighborhood just shy of two hundred. Regardless of the actual tally, I think we can agree it's a substantial list. More importantly, many of these biases are hard at work when we make decisions based on our views of the risks and rewards involved.

Imagine a cartoon in which the animated character has been faced with a tough choice of whether or not to do something. They're scratching their head or rubbing their chin, trying to determine the right move. Sitting on one shoulder is an angel. Or maybe it's a devil, depending on your perspective. Either way, they're holding a sign that reads "RISK." On the other shoulder is the devil, or angel, wearing a T-shirt with "REWARD" printed on the front.

Both of these encouragers are whispering in the ears of the undecided character, trying to make their case for why they represent the best option.

RISK is pleading, "Don't do it!" REWARD is urging, "Do it! Do it!"

More than likely, if this cartoon image came to life, turning into a real-world scene as we have watched happen in movies and music videos, the cognitive bias for this person would favor the idea that the potential prize (reward) of their decision is bigger than the perceived pain (risk).

Yes, we most often side with rewards, believing they exceed the risks involved. This is one of our many cognitive biases. The reward of something working out is worth taking the risk of it not working out. We're willing to accept punishment if we presuppose the benefit is most probable and worth it. There's no denying this represents a blind spot. This thinking isn't in our direct line of cognizance, but it's very real, not to mention extremely common.

Risk/Reward questions allow for a reduction of emotion in decision-making. If we can rationally determine risk and compare it to a realistic view of reward, we can make better decisions. Would anyone ever decide to do something when the risk outweighed the reward? Of course they would, but that's another issue altogether. Maybe I should rephrase the question....

Should anyone ever decide to do something when the risk outweighed the reward?

At a minimum, the risk versus reward calculation will lead to fewer bad choices, even if that number is disappointingly low. Ultimately, people are responsible for their own decisions. We, as Facilitators of Betterment, can only control so much. But navigating an assessment of risk versus reward helps people to manage their expectations. An individual might still go ahead with a bad decision, but they'll have a conscious awareness of its badness and be better prepared for the aftermath.

We, as a society, often make miscalculations and tell ourselves that a decision is worth it. We take on high levels of risk while believing, or hoping, that things will work out. The detrimental reality is that wishful thinking prevents us from accurately assessing the risk involved because of a systemic flaw in our thought process. Assessing risk is difficult when we don't believe negative outcomes will materialize. We find comfort in having faith about things finding a way to work out. They always do. Don't they? This cognitive bias gets us in a ton of trouble.

WHEN *DOES IT MATTER?*

Intuition will be your guide with this Question That Matters, like many others. When you sense anyone involved in the process misjudging the variables being factored into a determination, Risk/Reward questions are an ideal option to utilize. Perhaps you have a gut feeling they're underestimating risk. It could be that the reward they're anticipating is being overestimated. Or both could be happening. Another possibility is that what you're detecting is uncertainty, and they simply don't know how to properly gauge risk and reward.

We can't lose sight of the bias at play and the churning likely taking place below the surface, at a subconscious level. These questions can be used to explore clouded thinking by objectively examining the different variables and, therefore, reducing the amount of emotion influencing a decision.

If my earlier attempt to capture the essentials of this dynamic through a thought-up cartoon didn't hit the spot for you, perhaps I should attempt another illustration. Picture one of those old-school balances with the plates on each side hanging by a chain. No, those aren't scales. I checked first to be sure. Scales measure weight, while balances measure mass. So there! As Risk/Reward questions are asked, we're guiding participants through the mental exercise of putting information, in the form of answers, on each side. The end game, after all the answers have been placed, is to determine on which side of the balance it tipped, risk or reward. We do this when people need to either recalibrate their perceived estimates or when they need to get an initial reading on them.

HOW *IS IT ASKED IN A WAY THAT MATTERS?*

Once more from the cheap seats…we're really bad at answering the "Is it worth it?" question. Did I mention that already? Ad nauseam, you say? Got it.

I'll attempt a reversal of tone and put a positive spin on this reality. If we're able to support people in exploring such evaluations in a more tangible, pragmatic manner, they can find themselves in an improved position for success. How did I do? To make this happen, we can utilize Risk/Reward questions in formats representing two distinct methods.

The Integrated form incorporates risk and reward into a single, comprehensive question, asked in a way that challenges people to assess them simultaneously. Furthermore, the question calls for a comparison of both elements in one fell swoop. That might sound challenging and somewhat tricky. And there's legitimacy in those concerns, but the Integrated approach for Risk/Reward questions is a far cry from unworkable. In fact, reality says otherwise. This version of a Risk/Reward question should be asked in a nonchallenging manner, as an expression of genuine interest regarding the end results of possible consequences. We're showing care by asking people to pause for a moment and reflect upon how their decision looks on the balance sheet, so to speak. A cognitive bias could have steered them toward focusing on only one variable, either tunnel vision on the upside or dwelling only on the downside. This question forces people to consider both for a shot in the arm of perspective. Or this Integrated form could efficiently reinforce the calculation they've already processed by confirming that one variable actually does outweigh the other.

Using a Segmented approach, we break down the mattering into risk and reward variables. With risk, we need to give people a mechanism to appropriately quantify what's at stake with their pending choice. The natural tendency defaults to underestimating or lowballing the losses or costs involved. For reward, the slant is toward overestimating. We tend to inflate the perceived benefits of an outcome.

In both scenarios, we're looking to obtain realistic snapshots of each variable needed to make the calculation. As a Facilitator, we need to ask this Question That Matters in a way that puts objectivity into decision-making that's often fueled by emotion.

WHAT ARE SOME EXAMPLES OF IT MATTERING?

Risk/Reward questions have application within the many distinctive relationships we form in our various capacities. For the sake of putting those interpersonal dynamics in the context of this particular conversation, here are a few Facilitator-Participant ties that should be underscored:

Consultants-Clients
Coaches-Players
Sales professionals-Customers
Therapists and Counselors-Clients and Patients
Community leaders-Citizens
Business leaders-Employees
Teachers or Trainers-Students
Parents-Children
Coworkers and Teammates-Other Coworkers and Teammates
Friends-Friends
Managers-Staff and Team members
Mentor-Mentee
Executive coach or Life coach-Client

Facilitators can ask Risk/Reward questions in the spirit of guiding participants by ensuring the step they're about to take is indeed helping them get to a better place. Keeping these affinities in mind, we should go ahead and get the first example out of the way. It's sitting in front of us, frantically waving its hand, begging to be called on. This version of the question is glaringly obvious but needs to be stated, for the record:

How does the risk *of this option compare to the* reward?

The keywords were stressed so that even more glare is slapped on top of the obvious.

As I said, this example was a formality. But we won't stop there. Additional hypothetically posed questions of both Integrated and Segmented approaches should shed some light on putting this mental exercise into practice.

We highlighted this question at the beginning of the chapter, and it was also referenced as a pre-s'mores indulgence consideration. At its core, this is an Integrated form of asking if benefits exceed liabilities:

Is it worth it?

And here's a query that could be used to assess any major purchase: *Does the value justify the cost?*

Value means different things to different people, so I'll resist the urge to drag us into the weeds. But the point of this Integrated Risk/Reward question is to mentally place nonemotional objects on both sides of the balance.

Has anyone ever told you to grab a sheet of paper and create two columns for a decision you're struggling to make? You would put a plus sign at the top of the first column and the other one would get a negative sign. Then, the task is to write a list of the pros followed by the cons. At the end, you compare the lists. The problem that exercise is meant to solve: *Are you confident that the positives outweigh the negatives?*

And here's a template that could be used to evaluate the give-and-take of Risk/Reward:

Do you feel there is enough _____ to rationalize the _____ that could take place?

Those blanks could be filled with:

- Gain/Pain (Not a weightlifting reference, but I acknowledge the humor)
- Upside/Downside
- Profit/Loss

This two-birds-with-one-stone package is a fine way to go in the Integrated approach. But there are circumstances when you need a big rock for each bird, and that's when the Segmented version comes into play.

Now we're zeroing in on either risk or reward. If we were breaking down the first, obvious Integrated example into the different components, this is the way each could be expressed using the Segmented approach:

Have you considered all the risks involved with that choice and, if so, how do they look?

What about the rewards that could be gained?

The first question is meant to make sure risk isn't being undervalued. The other protects against overstating reward.

Each of the examples shared in the Integrated section could be compartmentalized in this way to direct attention where it's most needed. For practice, try breaking down all those previous examples. Go ahead, I'll wait…

Moving along, you'll remember we covered Range-finding questions in a prior QTM chapter. Did you see how I snuck a new acronym in there? My attempt at a crude experiment. I wanted to see if you could figure out what it meant, or if you cared, while also testing whether there was enough staying power for it to become part of our lexicon, like WIIFM. No way? Oh, well. I tried.

Range-finding and Risk/Reward questions can join forces. The Best/Worst combination in a Risk/Reward format is an effective method for testing the extremes of perceived outcomes. They help us understand the limits and boundaries people believe represent the potential effects of the decision they're contemplating. Putting these two types of questions together, the combo might look like:

What would happen if the worst outcome took place? (Risk)
If the best scenario played out, what would that do for you? (Reward)

Finally, after asking these questions, whether in the Integrated or the Segmented format, there's one final question that can be used as a form of checks and balances for any choice or determined course of action. This gut check stops the motion for a moment, allowing for reflection and a lessening of the influence of emotion.

Are you sure?

As an aside, we could dedicate a serious amount of time on this confirmational inquiry. It's a humdinger and could be a stand-alone confab in itself, but I'll show restraint for once. We'll leave well enough alone and call this extra credit for Risk/Reward questions. Time to move on. I have a knack for bringing the drama, right? What a cliff-hanger!

You might be saying, "That's not cool. Don't leave me hanging! Tell me more!"

Not happening. But what a great segue…

20

QUESTION THAT MATTERS #9

ANYTHING ELSE?

'm sure you've been breathless with anticipation while patiently awaiting an Isaac Newton reference. The long wait is over. You can breathe again.

Newton was a pretty smart dude. During his lifetime, around a half a millennium ago, he explained quite a few phenomena that had most everyone else in the world befuddled. My personal fave is Newton's First Law of Motion. It basically says that an object at rest will stay at rest and an object in motion will stay in motion, as long as nothing messes with it. Yes, there's more to his explanation of inertia, and I'm sure Sir Isaac would be offended by my rudimentary interpretation, but we must stay on task. I do want to bring your attention to a specific part of that statement:

An object in motion will stay in motion.

This speaks directly to momentum as an important force in the realm of Disruptive Discovery. Having already made several keynote appearances, momentum again makes its presence felt with our next deep dive into a question. As participants in the process provide feedback and share information, we can take advantage of this forward progress to obtain a greater amount of detail and achieve more depth. This capitalizing on inertia can be communicated using only a few words.

Anything else?

Of all the Questions That Matter, this one is by far the most self-evident. There are other phrasings that can be used—more on that later—but its lifeblood is sustained by seizing momentum and leveraging the dialogue already in motion. This is an unflashy but extraordinarily potent mode for keeping exchanges moving in the right direction and maintaining a steady flow of information to fill the knowledge funnel we can use for helping people as they work to solve their problems or make desired improvements.

I'm guilty of many foibles. Overcomplicating pretty much everything is high on that list. But out of respect for this wonderfully uncomplicated question, I'll do my best to avoid my all-too-familiar blunder. If I stray or deviate from this commitment to keep it simple, you can smack me in the back of my head. I see how that might be logistically challenging, so maybe just send some mean thoughts my way or write a nastygram. You know what I'm saying.

WHY *DOES IT MATTER?*

Less is more.

Hey, our first oxymoron! There have been several paradoxes and a slew of analogies, but oxymorons have been evasive, like a unicorn sighting. I feel so much better. Even though less being more defies common sense, it's an axiom that holds water. I'm also a proponent of the addition-by-subtraction school of thought. I've found these contradictive philosophies chock-full of wisdom.

However, in the arena of obtaining knowledge and insights through the answering of questions, less is NOT more. Nope, less is less. And, not to kick it when it's down, but less kinda stinks. Minimal details can leave us wanting. On the other hand, more kicks some booty. It's the founding principle of this Question That Matters. We want to be greedy, even gluttonous, about consuming information. To that end, "Anything else?" questions matter very much.

I just thought of a catchy saying to drive home this point. *With scant INFO, Disruptive Discovery DON'T GO!*

Ugh. Not good. I should probably stay in my lane and avoid the rhymes. Typing that anti-proverb gave my fingers a weird, tingly sensation. I need to get right back on the horse after such a debacle. Allow me to make amends by submitting that detailed responses are the substance of gaining a deeper level of understanding. That's more like it, even without the rhyme.

If we somehow overask this question and receive a surplus of information, we can put this challenge in the category of good problems to have. Our welcome predicament would turn into combing through the amassment of learnings accumulated and cradling those insights fitting of action. I'll gladly accept such an undertaking over the struggle of dealing with insufficient information anytime. But I'm here for you and, by enacting this technique in the proper moments, we greatly alleviate the need for navigating either lacking or excessive feedback.

WHEN *DOES IT MATTER?*

Keep this tool at your fingertips throughout the entire facilitation process. It could and should be used early, often, and on a continuous basis as you deem necessary. When listening to an answer, you might sense there's still "meat on the bone" that could lead to more knowledge. Offering an encouraging nudge in this situation is just the ticket.

A cracked open door for deeper exploration could present itself with a few different looks. In some cases, it's apparent there's more to say, but, for some reason, a friendly, gentle prodding might be necessary to keep their thoughts flowing. Maybe an assist is needed to get complicated ideas unstuck, reinforce your interest, or seek permission to keep talking.

Other circumstances could develop as a mild hunch that the amount of feedback to be gained is nearing an end. You just never know for sure when using this question as a mode of confirmation. Perhaps the tank is, as suspected, empty. Or you might unexpectedly stumble upon an opening of the floodgates of new information. In that case, the end result will give us more cards from which to assemble the best possible poker hand. If our attempt does fall flat because participants truly have nothing left to share, not to worry. No harm, no foul. That's totally fine, assuming we asked the question properly.

HOW *DO WE ASK IT IN A WAY THAT MATTERS?*

Reiteratively, this particular QTM (I'm not giving up) is relatively straight-forward, and we don't want to fall into the trap of overthinking mechanics or outsmarting ourselves. It's relatively low risk and disproportionately high reward. Why does that sound like a familiar mental calculation?

This isn't necessarily a case of what you say, but more about the subtle nuances of how you say it. While emboldening you to move forward with confidence, I also figured there were no drawbacks in offering a few constructive tips. Success or ineffectiveness in your pursuits will be influenced by two factors:

- **Sincerity**—Forward questioning progress is most likely maintained when high levels of this trust requisite have been demonstrated and are in place.

- **Timing**—That might sound like it belongs in the *WHEN* section of our review. However, I felt this element belonged in *HOW* because it represents more of a style or finesse call. You comic book fans out there can think of this perception as a Spider-Sense. By asking too early, we can squash the momentum that was built. Contrarily, waiting too long can make it tough to rekindle the fire if asked after starting to extinguish itself. The sweet spot clearly falls in the middle and isn't difficult to nail.

Those cautions were worth mentioning, but, once again, we shouldn't trip over ourselves with any unprovoked wavering.

WHAT *ARE SOME EXAMPLES OF IT MATTERING?*

There are several effective ways to ask people to expand on their commentary through "Anything else?" And sometimes those exact words are all that's needed. Remember, trying to get too cute with style points can lead to a preventable shooting of our own feet. In practice, this version of the question could either be used in the exactly stated manner or with a slightly more formal variation:

"Is there anything else you'd like to add?"

Other renditions embodying the crux of this ask can also be applied to leverage momentum. Apply originality in concocting customized alterations based on the nature of what you bring to the table and the uniqueness of the situation. Being creative isn't my strong suit but, just for kicks, I'm itching to attempt a handful of options in this bonus round:

Can you tell me more?

Statement form is also an option. Yes, we can ask statements by making them function as questions:

That's really interesting. Tell me more.

Now, back to example questions that are…questions:

Would you keep going with that thought?

Wow. What you just said is gripping. Could you elaborate?

Here are several Clarifying questions that also qualify as "Anything else?" They keep the dialogue moving, capitalize on forward progress, and help solicit more details.

Can you help me understand…

What do you mean by that?

A little while ago, we celebrated our first oxymoron. As a follow-up, I thought a paradox would be in order. Maybe I can think of a quick metaphor or analogy to complete the trifecta. That sounds like a lot of work, though, so I'm going to settle for offering this paradoxical thought…

Another way to ask this question is by saying nothing at all.

Deep, huh? But it isn't nearly as absurd as it sounds. That philosophical allegation is actually true because "Anything else?" can be asked nonverbally. All it takes is an inviting look of interest, and maybe even a subtle "bring it on" or "keep it coming" gesture with your hands.

That's all I've got for this chapter. What's that? Did you say something? Oh, you asked if I had anything else to add. Good one. You're funny.

For anyone keeping score at home, that's nine down, one to go. And an argument could be made for Question That Matters #10 being the granddaddy of them all.

I'm not exactly sure what makes the world go round. Maybe it's gravity. Ironically enough, Isaac Newton had a lot to say about gravity after that apple bonked him on the head. Gravity could be the explanation. Or, for all I know, gravity is a derivative of this giant rock we inhabit doing so much whirling. Either way, that's not really the point, and all this talk is making me dizzy. Our final question was made for these diagnostic moments and if whatever-the-cosmic-power-source ever loses its juice, this dynamo could be a backup generator capable of keeping the earth spinning for a long time.

21

QUESTION THAT MATTERS #10

WHY?

A single, lonely word followed by a question mark...but it packs a wallop.

Awesome is the adjective that first comes to mind and best depicts the character of this powerhouse. And just like that, I've asserted another special term I undeniably overuse, point taken. But this time I *will* back it up.

A variety of dictionary definitions for "awesome" are at our fingertips. You'll find some distinctions in the descriptions, but also quite a bit of overlap and commonality. Some of the most notable labels are impressive, daunting, inspiring, and causing admiration or fear. Awesome is quite a word, you must admit. It fits our guest of honor for this final Question That Matters chapter like a glove.

Please join me in welcoming our honorary guest, "Why?"

A one-syllable question, objection, statement, possibly even an expletive.

As a question, I freaking love it. Like as in the high school crush, heart-eyed, fatal attraction type of adoration. And I'm not alone. There are an overwhelming number of books, articles, and other resources out there that focus purely on this question. Many of them are brilliant. I mentioned

Simon Sinek before, and his book, *Start with Why*, fundamentally changed the way I see purpose and inspiration in *everything*. There are gobs more, and they can be found in superabundance. I recommend seeking out these reads and dipping into as many as possible. My goal isn't to recycle content that already exists. And I don't want to opine about this topic, adding yet another dissertation of "why" onto the already mountainous pile that has been previously distributed. That would be a waste of your time and, to be honest, wouldn't add any value.

My intention is to share the influential impression "Why?" has made on me. I'll attempt to disseminate what I've learned about the power of this question and the ways in which it can be used. If it's linguistically possible to ask anything a billion times, I've undoubtedly exceeded the quota.

We know young children use this query as an expression of curiosity. They ask "Why?" with anything and everything. My Daughters fit this profile, and they're nipping at my heels with a ravenous determination to smash any "Why?" records or lifetime achievement awards I manage to earn. I do find it interesting that when I ask the question it sounds profound, but when they ask…let me think…what's the opposite of profound?

In all fairness, I do encourage them to "why away." Most of the time, I grin on the inside when it happens. *Most* of the time. There's a certain music to my ears when one of my children asks such a mattering question. But there are other times when my reaction isn't quite as welcoming. Perhaps that's a byproduct of my mindset. Shame on me. Or perchance it's possible, even the slightest possibility, they could have posed the question for a better reason, at a better time, and in a better way. As a question-crazed dad, it's my sworn duty to continue teaching them, passing along everything I know about this question, and others, so that a positive difference can be made in their lives. Which brings us right back on track to where we started.

This is an invitation for you to listen in as I pronounce *my* take on "Why?" based purely on experiences and the way I've interpreted them into transferable takeaways. The only research, facts, and data used to formulate the ideas I'm passing along come directly from application of these learnings and other wisdom I've humbly borrowed from many sources. Microexperiments with general concepts performed over those one billion-plus times in the trial-and-error laboratories of my everyday life. I'm jazzed by what follows, but I'm also nervous about botching something so near and dear to my being. It feels as if I'm working out a trapeze act without a safety net. I hope you enjoy the show because, truth be told, heights scare the you-know-what out of me.

WHY DOES IT MATTER?

Let me get this straight. My charge is to explain why "Why?" matters? Or I need to solve the riddle of why "Why?" That's far-out, man. A black light, a lava lamp, and some of those psychedelic posters might be a groovy way to set the mood for this session. We're entering "I think, therefore I am" territory.

I'm just messing around. Though this metaphysical trek sounds like a ticket into a vortex of abstraction, there's a deceptive amount of logic involved. Getting our arms around "Why?" means understanding these key, and indisputably substantive, principles:

- Purpose
- Cause
- Reason

If you're champing at the bit to point out that cause and reason mean the same thing, I wouldn't be shocked. Yet you would be wrong. Ouch. That was rude. Let me back up and try a redo.

You would *not be correct*. Better?

There's a noteworthy differentiation between cause and reason that I'm obliged to disclose because a line has now been drawn in the sand. A cause produces an effect. It makes something happen. Reason supports a decision, idea, or opinion. Think of it as a justification for an action. This could appear to be some hairsplitting, but I think you'll see how this distinction plays out because stopping there would be a monumental disservice. We need to keep going with this train of thought.

To truly tap into the potential of "Why?" more depth is required.

Certainly there is value in knowing the purpose, cause, or reason of any situation. We can put that knowledge to work, no sweat. But what if there was more to the story? What if there was a story behind the story that was the *real* story? I don't know about you, but *that's* the story I'm streaming on Netflix. I should stop floundering around and lay out the concept that eloquently captures what I'm suggesting.

Core.

If something is core, it's at the center. Core is the most basic, fundamental, essential, important, innermost ingredient of anything. And… that…is…what…we…want!

Which would you prefer, purpose or CORE purpose? What's better to know, cause or CORE cause? If you had a choice between a reason or the CORE reason, I know which one you're picking. At least I hope so!

By asking "Why?" we position ourselves at a transcendent angle to understand core purpose, cause, or reason for whatever's the object of our discovery endeavors. This question doesn't just matter, it *really* matters.

WHEN *DOES IT MATTER?*

We must keep our eye on the ball in regard to situational context. This *Ode to Why* is all about strategic positioning of the question as a provocateur in the process. In Surface Discovery, reaching for any of the QTMs (sticking yet?) should be done sparingly. Such a level of progressive agitation should be reserved for situations calling for an urgency to push farther. This reality is especially pertinent with "Why?" There are many circumstances in which a more surface level, or mildly rooted, awareness of purpose, cause, or reason is sufficient. The demands are often more readily satisfied in those respective occurrences.

But those aren't the circumstances imploring you to spend time in our clubhouse of disruptors. Our gang revels in uncovering the real deal, the heart of the matter, and what makes something, or someone, tick. In these cases, digging to the core is the difference maker. To stress this point, I pulled together a rundown of the scenarios representing perfectly suited conditions in which "Why?" can be applied as a core finder:

- **Problem-solving** – Diagnosis through root cause analysis leads to identifying solutions that address the real issue.

- **Development areas** – Pinpointing the origin of a decision to improve certain skills can aid people in their pursuits.

- **Disconnected values** – Reconciling actions and behaviors with the standards, integrity, and character participants wish to personify shores up culture.

- **Confusion** – Lifting the clouds of disorientation resulting from not being able to figure something out cuts down on distractions and allows people to see with clarity.

- **Lack of buy-in or rumblings of disharmony** – Getting people aligned and on the same page is the cost of admission for any enterprise that people don't want to fail miserably.

- **Waning, broken, or absence of trust** – Validating sincerity when these red flags are detected during the process serves to grow, rebuild, or establish trust between all players and/or yourself as a Facilitator.

- **Apathy** – An infusion of passion, energy, or engagement when there's a shortage propels meaning and improves the forecast for advancement.

- **Underconfidence or overconfidence** – Strengthening perspectives or beliefs when lacking, improves the fortitude of individuals to make something happen. Softening their perspectives or beliefs when they need to be taken down a notch or two serves as a shot of reality, while also improving the fortitude of others to cooperate with that individual…before they disown them.

- **Codependency** – Empowering people to find solutions on their own, make mistakes, and teach themselves instead of relying on others are vigorous development exercises for them…and sanity savers for everyone else in the mix.

A myriad of settings can be routinely encountered in which this question would intensify learning. This list represents those most likely screaming for "Why?" due to the nature of the hurdles they represent in Disruptive Discovery and the depth of understanding required to jump over them. Er…I muddled my swing at dazzling symbolism…that should have read…the depth of understanding required to *tunnel underneath* them.

HOW *DO WE ASK IT IN A WAY THAT MATTERS?*

There are numerous forms this Question That Matters can take. To make them as digestible as possible, I've arranged them into the main buckets. Each of these categories represents its own technique for asking this type of question.

First, there is the self-described be-who-you-are, put-it-out-there approach. The most direct way to deliver a "Why?" question is…drumroll, please…"Why?" From there, step back and let your ask run the show itself. The response should take us to a deeper level of awareness and knowledge. And, for the most part, this information download is exactly what we're trying to achieve. Posing "Why?" prompts a progression from basic-level comprehension of purpose, cause, or reason to a more exhaustive, complete picture.

Now, if this is your chosen approach, there's a disclaimer in the fine print. Using this most concise form requires a pre-acknowledged trajectory. You must ensure there's no ambiguity with participants that could lead to either "Why what?" or an answer that addresses something other than what was intended. In other words, people need to know exactly what in the heck you're asking about.

Next, we should talk about rolling out an altered variation of the put-it-out-there natured method. Think of this format as "Why? with GPS."

This would be done by narrowing the focus. Ask questions that point to the different components of purpose, cause, or reason.

This version should be directed to a specific statement, idea, or suggestion that has been offered. A vague or blanket "Why?" question can lead to confusion, even frustration, depending on the circumstances and audience involved. If there's a need to acquire buried insights, we should be definitive about the orientation of our request.

Yes, "Why?" is a powerful one-worder of a question. But at times it can be more effective through a contraction in breadth, looking more like, "Why _____?" The blank space is obviously where you insert the specific area of concentration. A new toy with some assembly required. Catch my drift?

Finally, a more methodical, purposeful, multilayered avenue can work extremely well. Each round of "Why?" represents incremental new knowledge gleaned. This gradual search can help participants ease into deeper sharing without feeling overwhelmed by the task of finding the core from the get-go. You'll see an example of how this flows shortly, but the technique is "Why?" followed by "Why?" and on it goes.

Before moving into our closing section, there are a few more warning labels we shouldn't ignore with respect to the methodology of asking this question. Sorry. I'm just keeping it real:

- Remain watchful and diligent in how far you push. Or, more simply stated, know when to say when. Peel back enough layers, giving enough depth to discover the core. Attempting to dig deeper results in diminishing, potentially counterproductive, returns.

- Be careful with your tone. An improper delivery can sound condescending. Unfortunately, in some instances, that's exactly how people use it. They blurt out "Why?" as an inquiry, but, in reality, it's nothing more than a disguise—an objection dressed in a question's clothing. Predictably, the justifiable interpretation is processed as, "You're wrong!" Or an inappropriate inflection when posing this question, along with help from antagonistic verbal and nonverbal cues, can easily be misconstrued by anyone, leaving them feeling as if their ideas are invalid.

I must warn you to watch your step and be wary of another probable "Why?" pitfall. Take a seat because I need your full attention for this reality check. I'm just a beacon of hope, aren't I?

There's a profusion of sayings out in the stratosphere about how problems aren't problems. Instead, they're opportunities. That idea has been packaged into so many different clichés, they're a dime a dozen. With all those framed posters in offices and self-help greeting cards telling us about the yummy lemonade that can be made from squeezing lemons, there must be some merit to them. So, even if this makes me a mark, put me down for one of those "When life gives you..." tchotchkes. I'll need it for this next conversation. Stay tuned. Everything will make sense soon enough.

You're likely to encounter interactions in which people demonstrate difficulty with answering such an ostensibly unambiguous question. For reasons I'll strive to expound, when faced with "Why?" they either have great difficulty producing a cogent answer or, even worse, they *don't want to*. But the reply given in either of these situations is rarely true. And what exactly is that security blanket response?

"I don't know."

In fairness, this response is a legitimate possibility with any question and can absolutely be true. I'm simply pointing out that, of all the Questions That Matter, the highest probability of drawing an "I don't know" card happens when you've played "Why?" And my other point, cynical or not, is that people often know more than they think or are willing to share.

There should be a question simmering in your mind right now. I'm hopeful, and optimistic, that you're asking yourself, "So what?" Remember that guy? It's the right question and deserving of an explanation.

In past reviews of other Questions That Matter, we haven't invested a significant amount of time dealing with potential responses. In this case, we need to be proactive with our preparation because "I don't know" can be polarizing.

With polarizing, I'm advising that we, as askers, are susceptible to our own strong reactions when receiving this response. People exhibit varying responses when hearing "I don't know." Sure, some folks will perceive it as a harmless, face value reply and go on with eating their Lucky Charms. In contrast, there are people who could interpret this as a dreaded answer and stop in their tracks, wondering what to do next....

"Oh, you don't know? Uh, hmmmm. That's...not...what...I... Hmmmm. Really? You don't know?"

Even worse, there are others who, depending on the circumstances, are vulnerable to following up with a rebuttal resembling a kill shot. Parents, this might be a good time for you to look away...

"What do you mean, 'I don't know'? How can you NOT know? Of course you know. Just tell me!"

Nothing good will come from that diatribe. Begrudging acceptance, paralysis, showdown. Those are the possible reactions.

Not so fast. True to form, my propensity is a less popular option. In fact, it's the opposite. From my perspective, I've found not having the answers to be a liberating experience. I relish not knowing, sometimes bask in it. This assumes, of course, my state of unknowing isn't due to incompetence, laziness, negligence, or some other personal shortcoming. The *problem* with not knowing is, in my mind, an *opportunity* for growth, learning, and improvement. See? I told you I was buying into the problem/opportunity cliché extravaganza.

Not only is there untapped wonderment that can lead to prosperous new places, but pretending to have an answer is a recipe for disaster. The calamity might not be immediate, but fraud isn't something you want following you like toilet paper on the bottom of a shoe. It takes courage and humility to utter the words, "I don't know." But sometimes pride is worth swallowing.

To recap, in my observations, the answer "I don't know" is rarely true. Typically, that statement is a knee-jerk defense mechanism grounded in a reluctance to answer or an inability to fluently express thoughts. When the problem lies with articulation, it's all good. We can assume a supportive role and take them through the multilayered "Why?" exercise. With a reluctance to answer, we're facing a different challenge. This situation calls for us to focus our efforts on establishing, growing, or rebuilding trust. It could be that our sincerity is in doubt. Or maybe we just need to ask our "Why?" question in a different way. If making those adjustments doesn't move things forward, it's time to take a few steps back and implement what we know about trust in relationships.

I do highly recommend the anti-ambitious goal of not having all the answers in general. As Facilitators, we need to foster an environment that supports not knowing and encourages everyone involved to admit the same. It's a big step for any individual who truly wants to get themselves to a better place.

WHAT ARE SOME EXAMPLES OF IT MATTERING?

I'm thinking the best place to start is a swift overview of the examples we've already covered. The most direct manner in which to discover core purpose, cause, or reason:

Why?

A more targeted approach geared toward minimizing any possible confusion or vagueness:

Why _____?

We touched on the multilayered approach but didn't go into logistics. As a quick refresher, this meticulous exercise works to reach an adequate depth of understanding, one step at a time. I previously referenced children and thought it might be helpful to offer an illustration that combines the joys of parenthood with this "Why?" technique. Strangely enough, I have found that many of my learnings as a parent can be applied to professional and non-child-related personal situations. For your reading pleasure, I present to you a make-believe, or not-so-make-believe, exchange between parent and child to bring this method home, literally…

Child: *I don't want to go.*
Parent: *Why?*
Child: *Because it's stupid.*
Parent: *Why do you think it's stupid?*
Child: *Because nobody else is doing it.*
Parent: *Why do you say that?*
Child: *I've talked to all my friends and they don't have to go.*
Parent: *Why is that important to you?*
Child: *Because I wouldn't know anyone there.*
Parent: *Why does that upset you?*
Child: *Because it's a scary feeling to not know anyone.*
Parent: *Ah, OK. Can we talk about that?*

And there's always the more traditional Plan B…

Child: *I don't want to go.*
Parent: *Tough noogies. We paid a lot of money so you could do this thing. You're going and I don't want to hear any arguing.*

This almost always ends in tears and hurt feelings—for the parent. And to my earlier point, if you think that swapping the characters in these scripts with roles other than parent and child renders them obsolete, think again.

We also covered a comprehensive list of circumstances that represent a strong fit for uncovering core purpose, cause, or reason. Here are a few samples of "Why?" questions that could be used in some of those scenarios:

Last time our company rolled out this type of promotion, we know how everything played out. Why do you think these were the results?

Think of this as a reverse cause-and-effect inquiry. The effect is known, but the root cause needs to be explored.

Learning how to increase your emotional intelligence is an admirable goal. Why do you feel this will lead to enhancements in your relationships?

Recognizing what initiated an eagerness within someone to cultivate a new skill can heighten your effectiveness as a support resource in their venture. And I concede, with no argument, that this was a shameless, crowbarred plug for EQ. This is a personal hot button issue of mine and I have a longing for more of this skill in our world.

Why do you think this new platform will make life easier for your employees?

Getting the drivers of an idea to publicly explain its benefits to others involved promotes buy-in and getting on the same page.

Why do you feel that way about this plan?

A demonstration of sincere interest and concern can bolster trust building. There's a chance for a dual payoff by unearthing any obscurity necessitating lucidity.

There's no denying what they said in the meeting was undermining and harmful. Why do you think they said it?

Textbook application of empathy to address waning, broken, or absent levels of trust.

I see you're being cautious about committing to this decision. Why not give it a shot and see what happens?

Delivers a message of reassurance to fortify confidence when there's uneasiness, while incorporating a hint of Risk/Reward analysis.

The examples are limitless. Just think of any occurrence—past, present, or future—in which you want to gain a deeper understanding and weave "Why?" around it.

With that, we've come full circle. An insatiable craving to discover the purpose, cause, or reason for perhaps the greatest mystery in life could put "Why?" to the ultimate test…

Why was pumpkin pie invented?

Don't worry. I won't taint our champagne-deserving accomplishment of completing this QTM pilgrimage with my misguided infatuation for a genesis-baffling baked good. But it felt pretty darn satisfying to stick that landing.

Now, back to our legendary triumph. Overkill? I should say not.

We did it! That's a wrap! The epic conclusion of the 10 Questions That Matter franchise is in the books. There's still work to be done, but you should pause, take a big ol' breath, and smell those roses.

You fully possess an arsenal of tools, in the form of questions, that can make a positive difference in your professional and personal interactions. I don't hide from the reality that these methods are intended to upset the status quo applecart. But, as we have learned, the discoveries that result from these disruptions uncover the stuff that really matters. With this stuff in hand, you have the resources to help people get to a better place.

Dictionaries might want to think about including this description in their definitions of awesome. Wouldn't you say?

PART FOUR

PUTTING A BOW ON
DISRUPTIVE DISCOVERY

22

PULLING IT ALL TOGETHER

When we started to explore the 10 Questions That Matter, it felt like Super Bowl Sunday. All the energy, enthusiasm, hype, and buildup around Disruptive Discovery finally reached the pinnacle. It was time to step on to a bigger stage, and we set things in motion with Question #1, "What if?" For me, this beginning imitated the kickoff, when those thousands of cameras flash in unison. Now, here we are. The big game has been played, confetti is everywhere, and the MVP just proclaimed "I'm going to Disney World! Baba Booey!"

As a football fan, that was fun. I enjoyed this somewhat campy portrayal of how far we've come. Thanks for humoring me. Unfortunately, it was also a faulty depiction because, after the Super Bowl, the season is over. There is finality when the clock hits zero. Players clean out their lockers, coaches evaluate the season, and mascots take their costumes to the dry cleaners.

For us, the game never ends. Not only is there still much to be done with how to complete the Disruptive Discovery changeover, going from theory into practice, but then we take the field. We get out there and do it. That's *our* Super Bowl. I'll go one better…our Betterment Bowl. We've dug into many of the principal pieces in great detail. However, there are some integral concepts to address that will allow everything to gel and make the process more than words on a page. At the end of the day, if you don't have faith in the process or a clear path to start using this method, we're wasting our time. And I'm committed to not letting that happen. The objective, a polished championship trophy, is to see you doing your thing in the different corners of your life, helping people to help themselves. We're in this thing together. Once we put in the remaining work, we can enjoy another parade down Broad Street. I'll come back to that.

Before filling in those gaps and peeking ahead to where we're going, we should spend some time digesting where we've been. Authenticity has been discussed at length, but it can't take hold without a thorough understanding of content, to the point that it starts to become second nature. While learning by osmosis is often cited playfully, we haven't yet figured out how to make that reaction work in chemistry class. Our best bet is to keep reviewing all key concepts already pored over so that they permanently linger in our brain. Repetition is a key principle in learning, without requiring test tubes and safety goggles.

The Long and Short of It

If I told you most everything we've covered up to this point could be summarized on a single page, what would you say? Of course, I'm most intrigued by what you would say other than, "Why didn't you just do that in the first place and save me a ton of time? You stole precious hours from my life and I want them back!" No need to respond. I'll just pretend you did a backflip, followed by exclaiming something like, "You da man! I can't wait to see this eighth wonder of the world that will change my life. I'm eternally grateful."

I've put together a cheat sheet to accompany this condensed blueprint to boot. You probably don't need such a tutorial, but I sure do. Think of it as Disruptive Discovery Color by Numbers. And I love me some color by numbers, almost as much as invisible ink. Feel free to use this overview as you peruse Figure 1 (*see page* 185).

✔ Trust is the heart of Disruptive Discovery. It represents the starting point and, once established, must be maintained through the entire process.

✔ Trust isn't an emotion. It's a situational decision based on an assessment of three requisites:
- CAN you do it? (Capability)
- WILL you do it? (Reliability)
- WHY are you doing it? (Sincerity)

✔ Trust represents an ever-present *external* dynamic in these interpersonal relationships because it stems from the participants involved. The levels in play have a constant influence on the effectiveness of your efforts.

✔ We demonstrate trust through behaviors and actions. Empathy is the most effective approach with trust building.

✔ The best fits for being a Facilitator in the Disruptive Discovery process are with:
- Solving challenging problems
- Improving in a development area

✔ Adopt a Mutual Concern mindset.

✔ Determine the Opening that exists for stakeholders by evaluating where they *are* and where they *want to be*.

✔ Establish your specific purpose. It originates with your desire to help people get to a better place and is an *inner* dynamic. Purpose must be met with matching desire from all players.

✔ Begin Surface Discovery through asking the RIGHT questions. They meet the criteria of:
- Being relevant
- Applicability
- Appropriateness

✔ Move further into Surface Discovery by obtaining new information, knowledge, and insights:
  • Use Prerequisite questions
  • Continue refining our picture of the Opening with Current State and Aspirational State questions

✔ Utilize Attentive and Interactive Listening through:
  • Clarifying questions
  • Verbal and nonverbal communication

✔ Transition into Disruptive Discovery using a two-step exercise:
  • Recap of the Opening
  • Transition question

✔ Uncover the Stuff That Matters
  • The 10 Questions That Matter (Figure 2, *see page* 187)
  • Maintain authenticity. Do not use QTMs as tricks or tactics.

✔ Disruptive Discovery Understanding*
  • Package and communicate agreement to participants (Figure 3)

I'm now thinking I got caught up in the moment and overpromised on my deliverables just a tad because this one-pager didn't capture *everything* (not to split hairs, but "most everything" was the exact stretch goal). We've come way too far and invested too much mental energy for that to be remotely possible. This self-imposed assignment was to hit all the high points and put together a snapshot of the model. We can take a few steps back and enjoy the view from afar. I'm tempted to fire off the cliché about forests and trees, but I'll spare you that.

---

* We haven't gotten there yet. Hold your horses!

Figure 1 – The Disruptive Discovery Model

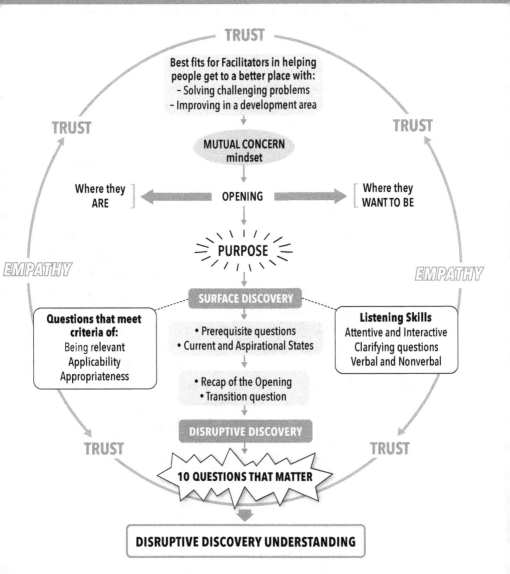

Disruptive		Discovery		Uncovering the Stuff That Really Matters
Stimulating change by challenging the status quo	**+**	Uncovering something new	**=**	*The process of gaining a deeper level of understanding with the intention of uncovering compelling learnings that motivate positive change.*

TRUST is a situational decision based on an assessment of three requisites:
✔ **CAN** you do it? (Capability)   ✔ **WILL** you do it? (Reliability)   ✔ **WHY** are you doing it? (Sincerity)

TRUST

Best fits for Facilitators in helping people get to a better place with:
- Solving challenging problems
- Improving in a development area

TRUST   TRUST

MUTUAL CONCERN mindset

Where they **ARE**   ←   **OPENING**   →   Where they **WANT TO BE**

PURPOSE

EMPATHY   EMPATHY

SURFACE DISCOVERY

Questions that meet criteria of:
Being relevant
Applicability
Appropriateness

- Prerequisite questions
- Current and Aspirational States

- Recap of the Opening
- Transition question

Listening Skills
Attentive and Interactive
Clarifying questions
Verbal and Nonverbal

DISRUPTIVE DISCOVERY

TRUST   TRUST

10 QUESTIONS THAT MATTER

DISRUPTIVE DISCOVERY UNDERSTANDING

This is as close as we get to an instruction manual. The process is nontechnical, so step-by-step directions wouldn't be fitting. It's not like we're assembling furniture, for Pete's sake. (Who is that Pete fella anyway?) So many unpredictable elements are involved. After all, we're dealing with people and the complexities of interpersonal relationships. I'll take savviness over a handbook as a practical compass for the intersections involved in the process, pointing to which turns to take and flagging those to avoid.

Nonetheless, all kidding aside, I wholeheartedly hope there will be a day in the not-too-distant future when these figures and the quick-reference flowcharty guide will look tired and worn from so much use. Well, would you look at that! It's past time to punch the clock and get back to work on filling in those gaps.

As I mentioned, there's more you need to know to transform this model from a really slick-looking diagram into a living, breathing mechanism for positive change. What follows is the lowdown I need to divulge before turning you loose. Think of this as a thrival, not survival, kit of functional tips and addendums for this method we continue to piece together.

An Endless End Result

The final destination in this process is elusive. Or is it an illusion? A mirage? I wanted so badly to nail a profound, thought-provoking idiom, but to no avail. So much for taking a crack at using imagery to point out that the place we're trying to go isn't a place at all. Disruptive Discovery is a continuum. It isn't a black-or-white proposition with a clear-cut beginning, middle, and end. The finished product is relative, subjective, a moving target.

It should go without saying that getting our arms around trying to measure the success of such amorphous exploits can be challenging. But I said it anyway. Without a plan, we can find ourselves running on a treadmill, which is great cardio but sure to have us wind up exactly where we started, only sweatier. Furthermore, how do we keep tabs on our results in getting people to a better place? I say without an ounce of hesitation that it can be done. Distance traveled and arriving at certain destinations along the way can be tracked as advances made in the degree of what we come to understand.

Figure 2 - The 10 Questions That Matter

By asking this type of question...	*You are helping people uncover what matters by...*
#1 – What if?	Envisioning the future by predicting how potential outcomes could play out.
#2 – So what?	Challenging relevance, substance, or potential for impact.
#3 – Range-finding	Expressing expectations based on the extreme boundaries of their experiences.
#4 – Dare to Dream	Considering possibilities without the limitations of reality or actual events.
#5 – The Other Side	Gaining a complete picture by viewing situations through more than one vantage point.
#6 – Impetus	Identifying the driving forces leading to their motivations.
#7 – Narrative	Using storytelling and anecdotes as a means to increase the flow of value-rich information.
#8 – Risk/Reward	Rationally comparing downside versus upside with a reduction of emotion in their decision-making.
#9 – Anything else?	Leveraging momentum to continue the sharing of information so that important details are not excluded from the process.
#10 – Why?	Exploring a deeper understanding of the core purpose, cause, or reason.

This might make some folks tremble because appraising levels of understanding isn't your traditional, concrete metric. My counterargument is that a measurement is a measurement, even if it's devoid of data in a spreadsheet, dollars on a financial statement, or pounds on the scale. Auditing forward progress or regression is plausible. Within my primitive intellect, there are different forms of measuring status.

For example, moving from Surface Discovery into Disruptive Discovery isn't as simple as brilliantly wording a randomly selected QTM (I can be very persistent) and firing away. No, that transition needs to be grounded in conspicuous affirmative movement. Such progress becomes bona fide when something remarkable happens in our interactions with others… understanding. Once we sufficiently *understand* the Opening that exists and feel there is enough distance between Current and Aspirational States, our intuition gives us a green light to proceed into Disruptive Discovery. We then incorporate what's *understood* into a well-timed Transition question. From there, the choice of a Question That Matters should be directly connected and relevant to the *understandings* we're trying to build on.

Understanding. It's the rock-solid basis of Disruptive Discovery that truly makes uncovering what really matters possible. And without authentic understanding, it's almost impossible to help people identify for themselves those insights that ultimately make the difference in enabling them to arrive at a better place. We're trying to determine what's real and cut through the noise, fluff, and smoke screens. Understanding. Understanding. Understanding. Did I say understanding? Thankfully, that process never ends, and for good reason.

Using the Proper Cadence When Asking Questions That Matter

Again, we don't have instructions to follow, so this is all about flying with the instruments you're developing. The cadence, or flow, that's adapted in your question-answer exchanges will have a say in their efficacy. According to my family, as I vented earlier, mine apparently leaves much to be desired. My qualifications for giving advice in this department might be suspect, but I do know it's deserving of attention.

After receiving a response, it's important to ask ourselves, "How did *that* go?" Look for discomfort or uncertainty. If either are observed, the concepts and suggestions we covered in the *HOW* section of each QTM can be put into play. And I can't overstate that listening skills are critical.

If the response points to progress through more understanding, we keep going, we keep listening, we keep learning. But recognize that relentlessly blasting through a list of questions isn't a viable option, nor should it even be a temptation. If you're authentic, the questions you decide to ask and the way you respond to the information shared will be much more effective. And with genuineness, staying true to your purpose, it becomes a natural process. It will both feel and be received as unforced.

Different types of follow-up questions keep the conversation moving or change the pace. Selecting the specific question to use at any given time is a skill that will emerge over time. A questioning style will become ingrained in you. Lots of lessons will be learned from successful attempts. And even more lessons will be learned from those that are unsuccessful.

Also, a certain synergy can emerge with the Questions That Matter. They can build on or feed off one another. Combinations can be devised, as referenced in previous chapters. And, in some cases, there's a seamless fit between certain questions.

As a refresher, earlier we applied a "What if?" format when asking Dare to Dream and The Other Side questions:

What if you could have anything and everything you want?

If some unexpected twists take place, should we anticipate any disadvantageous outcomes?

Or we utilize "Why?" as a follow-up for different QTMs. For example, a customer is telling you they're happy with their current vendor. Consider these Range-finding/"Why?" combinations:

What do you like best about the service they provide? That's interesting. Can you tell me why that's so important?

If you had to pick one thing, what's an area in which you'd most like to see improvement? *And why did you put this area at the top of your list?*

These types of questions and so many others we've examined are yours for the taking. Grab a handful. You've earned the right.

An Inconvenient Truth

I have a habitual tendency to learn lessons the hard way. Unfortunately, the path along what I keep referring to as my WHY has been littered with oodles of punches to the gut in the form of those learnings. In my experiences, a particular life lesson stands out as extra tough. Misery loves company, so pull up a chair.

A long list of trials and tribulations have led me to realize a harsh reality involved with trying to help people. I finally conceded to this realization after dragging myself, kicking and screaming, through many heartbreaking years. In Chapter 9, we talked about the need for matched motivation when establishing purpose for your Disruptive Discovery scenarios. This came on the heels of sharing an epiphany about inspiration and other sage reflections (more of those are coming soon!). But these are points worth revisiting, restating, and driving home. Here's the deal…

Having a desire to help people get to a better place is admirable. But Disruptive Discovery doesn't work unless everyone involved shares an equal desire for getting to that destination. Participants, players, and stakeholders must possess a sense of urgency to solve challenging problems or to improve in a development area. It can't be a one-way street. What's the harsh reality? Spit it out, right?

The life lesson is twofold and intertwined. First, I've found my most common source of disappointment to be unmet expectations. Second, people often fall short of expectations. Therefore, I've dealt with a lot of disappointment.

But the bitter pill so difficult for me to swallow isn't where you

---

*Notice, that was a somewhat sneaky technique for putting a positive spin on a Worst question.

probably think I'm going. There's been a lot of coaching between me and myself to correct this bad wiring in my subconsciousness. I've cut way, way down on the amount of blaming other people for expectations not being met in these situations. Most of the time, I'm proud to say the blame now goes to the person solely responsible for those expectations...me.

At some point, the convenience and ease of blaming other people for falling short of *my* expectations has *Groundhog Day* written all over it. Pointing a finger at someone else for the disappointment I feel at not fulfilling expectations I imposed on them is beyond unfair. They weren't looking to have anything dumped in their lap in the first place. I just assumed the help would be welcome. You know what they say about assuming? It leads to self-inflicted wounds. Isn't that how the saying goes?

When facing a situation with lopsided desires or expectations between you and others, I suggest choosing to remove yourself or, if avoidance isn't an option, addressing the disparity head-on. And for circumstances with mismatches more one-sided than lopsided, feel free to run for the hills. The chances are that it's not your fault and trying to make chicken salad will result in frustration for everyone.

Take it from me, a dupe who's far from a beginner with these missteps, and make the less valiant choice to avoid unnecessarily playing savior. On a more positive note, I'm thrilled to report this self-awareness has led to much less disappointment in my worlds. Just sayin'.

The "Mattering Filter"

That's right. A Mattering Filter. It's a real thing. Well, not quite yet. I just fabricated it. After I get a patent, build a manufacturing plant, and crank up the assembly line, they'll be mass-produced. That sounds like a lot of work and, on second thought, is an ill-conceived plan, so maybe there's another way to accomplish what this innovation was meant to do.

The general idea is that some stuff matters and other stuff doesn't matter much, if at all. For something to "matter," it must have substance, significance, and consequence. The Questions That Matter serve as wayfinders for us in this regard. To stay with the equipment analogy, think of those questions as a drill with different bits. They use various forms of disruption as a means to penetrate through the surface layers of any discovery opportunity so that we can start concentrating on the areas with meaning.

Based on that proposition, haven't we already learned what matters by facilitating dialogue with those questions? Yes, we have. But now the time has come for going a step further with our inquiry to uncover what's most pressing so that we can understand...

What *really* matters?

Enter the need for a Mattering Filter. And building one from scratch isn't necessary. This wheel has already been invented and is readily at our disposal. A Mattering Filter separates the stuff that's worthy of action from the greater population of stuff that doesn't necessarily require further attention, in that moment. What's a filter anyway? A piece of equipment or an appliance? A device? I'm starting to contest my own analogy. But we were jibing with it, so let's look straight ahead and pretend that didn't happen.

In some way, shape, or form, all the Questions That Matter are also robust filters for making these verdicts. They can act as a de facto double-filtration system. To demonstrate how this might look in practice, here's a sampling of questions incorporating different approaches that represent the embodiment of a Mattering Filter. Play along and see if you can recognize the specific QTM type for each of these examples:

What would happen to our service model with that change in personnel?

Why is this decision so important to your family?

If you do nothing to address that unhealthy relationship, how could it effect the interactions with other people in your network?

How does pushing ahead with this proposal help both our company and the customer?

Are you confident that the short-term feeling of gratification justifies the potential backlash that could arise with making this commitment?

As you can see, some of these questions could be interpreted as insensitive, dismissive, or even confrontational. But they're a spin-off of ideas and subject matter already uncovered during the process. This is also a perfect time to reinforce the power of intentions. By asking these questions with the intention of pushing resources and attention in a beneficial direction, they're more likely to be perceived in a positive manner by the individual or group involved. With self-serving mindsets or insincerity, the reception will likely be less warm and inviting.

In some cases, a Mattering Filter isn't necessary. The consequences have already been uncovered, good or bad, and can be seen clear as day. Action is required. We just need to find a big enough box and some pretty wrapping paper.

Packaging the Stuff That Really Matters

Disruptive Discovery is a process, first and foremost, and this label has been well documented since our embarkment. There are other appropriate characterizations, such as a journey, an adventure, a quest, an expedition, a pilgrimage, or an odyssey. Most have already been used, and I missed the boat by not stoking my flair for the dramatic with others. Regardless of the selected descriptor, Disruptive Discovery can be cumbersome and exhausting for everyone involved.

Don't misunderstand my point. The experience we're inviting people to engage in is exhilarating. A jolt of energy mobilizes us from the beginning and continues throughout the duration. However, depending on what's discovered in the process, combined with the overall nature of the problem or development area, stakeholders might feel drained, overwhelmed, or encounter sources of anxiety at some points. As adept Facilitators of Betterment, we have a responsibility to mitigate those emotions as they are observed. And we certainly have an obligation to calm any such lasting sentiments after the smoke begins to clear.

Basically, it wouldn't be acceptable to stir things up and then place the burden of sorting through the clutter on the shoulders of everyone else. Making sense of everything discovered is a collaborate effort. We must own and cherish this phase of Disruptive Discovery. Once all the collective learnings have been properly filtered and we've deciphered what really matters, the resulting understandings are crystal clear...to *us*. But these compelling insights must be organized and communicated to the other involved parties in a way that allows for what follows, notoriously known as next steps. This requires an exercise in cerebral and verbal packaging.

I believe in the intrinsic value of presentation. Window dressing, garnish on the plate, and an ironed shirt all have their place. At the same time, quality-rich content is our top priority, and making our results look like eye candy can't happen at the expense of substance.

Outlining a buttoned-up format would be right on time, so I should pull out my Johnny-on-the-spot costume. Or I could just put on my trusty game face and propose a standard structure in which we can rally around as an ideal starting point. Heading along that path, perspective must be maintained and common sense allowed to prevail with constantly unfolding interpersonal dynamics. We should avoid the trap of coming across too clinically, too rigidly. Any suggestions on how to illustrate a layout that would accomplish these objectives? Yes, another visual! You took the words right out of my mouth. They get me fired up too.

Take a look at Figure 3 (*see page* 195). This template is a framework for proper positioning of the understandings achieved through Disruptive Discovery. I almost titled this a covenant, but that seemed to carry an immoderately intense tone. Because understanding has been a running theme and this is technically an agreement between two or more people, there's no sense in deviating. And instead of continuing with "package," let's pivot and refer to this format as a Disruptive Discovery Understanding.

As with other intricacies we've discussed, your style and personality play a prominent role in communicating the stuff that really matters in a concise and comprehensible manner. Remain consistent in keeping with the environment that has gotten you here. We often hear the phrase, "It's not what you say, it's how you say it." That's only a half-truth. For the sake of this exercise, the most suitable saying should be…

It's what you say and it's how you say it.

Figure 3 - Disruptive Discovery Understanding

✔ Summary of what matters in relation to the specific problem-solving opportunity or development area
  • *Based on learnings uncovered during the entire process*

✔ Highlight what REALLY matters
  • *Refined short-list of those most compelling discoveries*

✔ Statement capturing what would be gained by successfully addressing actionable items
  • *Incorporate a sense of urgency around their desire to make a positive change*

✔ Check for affirmation
  • *Expectations are either established or refused based on their level of Agreement/Disagreement and Buy-in/Pushback*

The Hidden Treasure

Things are not always what they seem. And stumbling across the unanticipated is sometimes the pleasantest of surprises. It would be logical to surmise the conveying of understanding, as the culmination of everything we've painstakingly reviewed with this model, would be an eminently coveted prize. And I'll say nothing to downplay or diminish the worth of an agreement we labored to create with our collaboration co-conspirators. However, I'd like to interject a supplementary take on how to enjoy even more fruits.

The legacy I so wish for Disruptive Discovery, in addition to its unique ability for helping people get to a better place, is that of a wake-up call for nudging people out of their comfort zone so they engage in new, fresh conversations. This would be the haul of loot sitting in the hidden treasure chest, waiting to be found. From those conversations, a deeper level of understanding can thrive. Game-changing insights emerge during the phases, activities, ongoing trust building, question-and-answer sessions, and subsequent dialogue. Relationships flourish and people begin to prioritize seeing what's important through a diverse lens. The process itself is where it's at. We share experiences in which growth takes place, regardless of the outcome.

But what about all the tangible results? Oh, I would never forget about those guys. Unthinkable. Unimaginable. Unfathomable. They're the thick and heavenly layers of icing on the towering, sumptuous cake. A cake from which everyone involved with your Disruptive Discovery facilitation will cut an obnoxiously large piece and eat with a gratified smile.

And it would be criminal of me if I failed to mention who should get the first serving. That piece goes to you, the Facilitator. As everyone is stuffing their face with cake, nothing would make me happier than seeing you wearing the biggest smile in the room.

If any leftovers remain and, by chance, someone happened to save me the slab that has a disproportionate amount of frosting, it would be impolite of me to say, "None for me." I have a thing for cake. Desserts are a weakness of mine to the point of being an addiction, maybe even a vice. I haven't met many I didn't instantly befriend. The only exception is when a perfectly delectable sweet somethin' is ruined by unnecessary fruit, especially any type of drizzle. What's up with drizzle anyway? I'm in the minority with my fruit-on-dessert opposition, and it's probably safe to say you disagree with me too. I don't blame you. But maybe at least make an effort to see where I'm coming from before booing or making fun of me. You could try walking in my shoes...no, check that...you could try eating cake with my fork. There's a name for that skill.

What's it called again? I'm drawing a blank.

23

MORE ON EMPATHY

J ust when you thought it was safe to go back in the water, there's that word again. You're probably familiar with the Rule of 7. It's an old marketing term stating that people need to hear something a certain number of times for that message to stick and for them to take action. Do you want to hazard a guess on how many?

I'd like to propose a different rule for empathy. Let's call it the Empathy Rule of Infinity. I'm not exactly sure how many times the word has been typed up to this point, but, because you brought up marketing (or was that me?), I can assure you it needs even more advertising. I honestly don't think the law of diminishing returns applies to empathy. No matter how many times we talk about its importance, too much will never be enough.

Throughout this journey through Disruptive Discovery we've been traveling together, empathy has been along for the ride. Whether riding shotgun during the discussion of an empathy-dependent topic or sitting in the backseat, taking a less headlining role in others, this partner has been road-tripping with us, and for good reason. Without empathy, Disruptive Discovery would struggle to perform at the optimum levels we aspire to reach.

In Chapter 6, I got a little preachy and talked about practicing empathy with trust building. It has also been referenced at various times when exploring different aspects of Surface Discovery and the Questions That Matter. There was the analogy that empathy is a muscle that can be strengthened.

Yikes! I just had a flashback and recalled suggesting that you join a gym known as Club Empathy and start an exercise routine. And did I have enough nerve to suggest Empathator as the name of a made-up machine? Forgive me. What's done is done and I can't put that toothpaste back into the tube. But maybe those moments of temporary insanity demonstrate my passion. At the risk of sounding even preachier, I'll make a bold statement...

Empathy is one of the most powerful forces in the universe.

Those aren't empty words or an exaggeration. I would put it at #3 on the list, which is still way, way up there. My own Forces in the Universe Power Ranking System looks like this:

1. Love
2. Laughter
3. Empathy
4. Self-confidence
5. Gratitude

I'm fully aware that declaring any force as the most powerful in the universe is completely subjective. My ranking system has no real weight beyond an opinion from the peanut gallery. And I'm quite certain that Yoda or any superhero from the Marvel Universe would take exception to my list. But this is my book, not theirs.

Anyway, the reason I feel so strongly about the weightiness of empathy is because human beings are social creatures. Like it or not, we rely on one another and the interactions that happen among us. Higher levels of empathy lead to stronger relationships. I don't know how to make it any clearer and it's not even debatable. In our personal worlds, for example, empathy allows for gaining an understanding of what friends and family members are experiencing in their lives. From a professional standpoint, empathy leads to our becoming viewed by coworkers and colleagues as a collaborative, receptive resource when an important task needs to get done. In both personal and professional scenarios, those demonstrating empathy become invaluable, and bonds can be formed that are difficult to break.

Because of its influence in so many interpersonal dynamics, I felt it necessary to dedicate a whole chapter to empathy. This is an opportunity for us to take a deeper dive into a few concepts with which you've already become somewhat familiar. But, as you probably anticipated, I'll do my best to broaden your empathy horizons by positioning new knowledge through a few insights you might not have been expecting. Because those are always good times, just like a surprise party.

The Secret Sauce for Trust

We have repeatedly talked about the importance of trust in Disruptive Discovery. Trust is not only a starting point of the discovery process but is also fundamental to it. That means it's an ongoing, foundational presence in your relationships with all participants that doesn't dissipate, not ever. The ebbs and flows of trust either galvanize or suffocate your efforts to help people get to a better place.

The manner in which we build trust is also a continuous, never-ending process. There are many methods and concepts for trust building, but, as I have unabashedly repeated and reinforced, empathy is the bomb. We would be wise to reexamine the three requisites and questions that others are asking themselves when determining the level of trust to grant in a specific situation. This time, I'll offer some additional thoughts on what's happening in the background as it relates to empathy.

✓ *Are you capable—CAN you do it?*
- People associate empathetic behaviors, such as asking questions and listening, with competence. A stronger belief in your skill level equates to higher perceived capabilities.

✓ *Are you reliable—WILL you do it?*
- Demonstrated empathy gives others a feeling that "we're in this together" because of an emphasis on their interests and not yours alone. This togetherness vibe promotes a sense of reliability.

✓ Are you sincere—WHY are you doing it?
  - When practicing empathy, people are less likely to question your intentions. Expressing genuine interest, being present, and displaying authenticity delivers a strong message of sincerity.

Empathizing can give a boost of confidence leading to or further supporting affirmative answers with any or all of these trust-determining factors.

I'm hoping that was a painless concept to fathom. Which means it would only make sense to mix it up and follow with a concept that's a common misconception. At least, conceptually speaking.

Don't Confuse Sympathy with Empathy

Those words are often treated as if they have the same meaning. As a result, they're frequently used incorrectly. They sound similar and have common roots in feelings. But they have differences that exist at very fundamental and significant levels.

Sympathy is a feeling or an emotion. It's a way of expressing concern for someone else. It's a conscious recognition of how another person is feeling. The term is most often associated with unfortunate circumstances.

Empathy is an *awareness* of the feelings or emotions other people are experiencing. It's the act of trying to internalize a situation in a way that helps to understand how it's being experienced by someone else. You're attempting to see the world through their eyes or walk in their shoes, as those popular simplifications go, and I've already mentioned a few times. I tried to come up with my own expression but figured people were fond of those explanations for a reason, right?

The hope is that awareness matures into understanding. If you have a similar shared experience with another person, awareness is likely already in place and understanding can occur instinctively. For example, a personal or professional loss could be a source of commonality. Without such a bond, arriving at understanding might be dependent on mindful effort.

It should be noted that neither sympathy nor empathy are reserved exclusively for undesirable situations. Although this is the context routinely used for both. Due to the diligence and resolve involved, it's significantly easier for most people to sympathize than empathize. But if this is an area in which you'd like to improve, fear not. It can be done...with some dedication and hard work.

Becoming More Empathetic

Empathy can be learned. I'll say that again: Empathy can be learned. We can strengthen our capabilities in that area. Growth can be achieved in this life skill. Enough build-up, it's time to walk the talk.

Allow me to pass along a few suggestions I've encouraged others to try, myself included, that have yielded positive results. These are exercises aimed at advancing empathy skills:

- Get uncomfortable by putting yourself out there in new circles and networks
- Practice replacing statements with questions
- Stretch your curiosity limits
- Explore your biases
- Work on catching any judgmental thoughts before they take hold
- Welcome your differences with others instead of avoiding them, especially diversity of thought
- Form a habit of reminding yourself that appearances can be deceiving

Any and all these acts will get you headed in the right direction. Some are more challenging than others and will require pushing yourself to accomplish such an earnest objective. However, there's one basic practice missing from this list. It's an activity essential to developing empathy capabilities. If you were on a deserted island and were only allowed one means to increase your empathetic capacity, the selection should be a breeze.

Listening.

You get the irony of trying to listen more when stranded on an island by yourself, right? Regardless, do more of it. You can't overlisten. Integrate droves of Attentive and Interactive Listening praxis into your relationships. Make those listening practices deliberate focal points in future exchanges of all sorts. Over time, less effort will be required as they morph into habit. And I'm not using the term "morph" from a biological standpoint. But now that you mention it...

The Science of Empathy

Many years ago, I found myself sitting in a room, having an innocuous conversation with several people, and the topic somehow switched to politics. Normally, I would run from these unfortunate, no-win nightmares, but this was one of those company "social" events after a long day of meetings. You know, the "social" events with coworkers and the bigwigs above you on the corporate ladder. Such a relaxing and genuine environment, in which the alcohol is flowing, everyone is just being themselves, there are no hidden agendas, and nobody would ever think to say or do anything with the primary goal of making themselves look good or advance their careers. I mean, these "social" events are always exactly as advertised.

I acquiesce that was exorbitant cynicism, even by my own standards.

Anyway, I was a young buck in the early stages of my career and figured I would just go with the flow and do my best to blend with the group during this proceed-with-caution conversation. Plus, I couldn't leave because I was bumming a lift back to the hotel with a driver who was fully dialed into this utterly work-appropriate conversation. Hey, I like to have a few drinks, OK? Buddying up with a designated driver was very responsible of me. This is only of consequence because poor, innocent me was pretty much stuck with nowhere to hide.

Why I remember so many of the details is because there's a happy ending to this story. I learned a valuable lesson that proved to be a life changer for me. The ringleader of this powwow had one of those big titles that hypnotizes others into only saying the things they think that person wants to hear. For some reason, he noticed my wallflower act and wasn't going to let me off the hook. For some other reason, he decided there were dire political questions in which life was no longer worth living without knowing my stance. So, the hammering away befell me.

Even as an ambitious go-getter, I never had the aptitude for joining in hollow, obligatory dialogue meant to appease others. Man, how I wish I had that ability. But I didn't have it then and placation is still on my shopping list of missing talents. As a result, I responded to his loaded inquiries by grabbing the first virtue I could find in my repertoire. I answered them honestly.

In this line of questioning, we kept getting back to the same place. He would ask me about an issue and I would explain my views...the two of them. I was giving my perspective from both sides because, well, that's how I see the world. This frustrated our leader, but he wouldn't let it go. He kept pushing, challenging that it wasn't possible to have multiple perspectives on one political topic. Have an opinion. Take a side.

As luck would have it, an individual I admired very much at the time was also unwillingly suckered into this wildly germane work-related conversation. He and I were in the early stages of building a relationship I cherish to this day. This special soul is one of my greatest mentors and, to be honest, I wouldn't be writing these words right now if it weren't for his influence in my life.

At the end of this regrettable and nonsensical back-and-forth, after everyone dispersed to resume "socializing," he walked over and told me something using the most impeccable timing and style. The exact words were, "You have the gift of mirror cells." I couldn't hold back the biggest of smiles because it was an honor to receive this compliment from someone I held in such high regard. I said, "Thank you, that really means so much to me." Walking away, filled with an overflowing sense of pride, I asked myself the gorilla-in-the-room Clarifying question that's probably on your mind right now.

What the heck was he talking about?

The word I used then was a little more colorful than "heck," but I'm still trying not to offend any readers. I'd never heard of mirror cells and had no clue what in the world they were. Should I have jumped for joy, or was this an infestation for which I should call an exterminator? Did I need an antibiotic? Newly fixated on learning more about mirror cells, I hesitantly performed some research. I was worried about an imminent bursting of my bubble as I began nosing around but became pleasantly surprised, and riveted, by those findings. The knowledge learned has stuck with me over the years, and I thought it would be worth passing along. But in the ongoing spirit of full disclosure, I'll also offer a warning. Things are about to get somewhat textbookish and nerdy, but only for a bit.

Lo and behold, there *are* such things as mirror cells and they are fascinating. As far as scientific discoveries go, I'd put them in the relatively modern category, dating back only a few decades. The proper technical name is mirror neurons. As a proper technical kind of guy, I'll proceed accordingly.

Our brains are jam-packed with tons of cells and neurons stuffed into all of that magnificent gray matter. A neuron is a special type of cell that transmits impulses throughout our central nervous system and to our muscles. Did you know that we have around 100 billion neurons in our brains? Dumb question. Of course you knew that obscure biological fact and I apologize for insulting your intelligence.

Basically, neurons react to everything we encounter. When we're faced with something taking place around us, a stimulus, they talk to one another and send commands leading to body movements. They also communicate with one another when processing information. That's where a special group of cells get involved...mirror neurons. They respond to stimuli we're experiencing, but they also have similar reactions to external stimuli. In other words, when we see someone else faced with any stimulus, our mirror neurons process a reaction as if it were happening to us. Our brain partakes in a mimicry experience and thus allows us to learn through a form of imitation.

The brain doesn't stop there—not even close. It continues processing, now shifting its attention toward the other person's reaction to those stimuli. In theory, this allows us to also experience the same emotions and feelings, as witnessed by their response. Do you agree this is riveting stuff?

If you aren't on the edge of your seat, I get it. Just know that I'm doing my best to make this as unboring as possible.

The relationship between mirror neurons and empathy makes perfect sense when you take into consideration the building blocks we've been putting into place. We described empathy as an awareness of feelings and emotions experienced by other people. Mirror neurons allow our brains to process situations experienced by others as if we were also experiencing them. This is a built-in mechanism for "walking in their shoes." And there you have it: the most frequently spoken definition of empathy.

You might be wondering why empathy is so rare if these mirror neurons are scientifically proven to exist. Shouldn't everyone be oozing with it?

Unfortunately, this is where my amateur-level credentials get exposed and my knowledge of this biological phenomenon comes to a screeching halt. Plus, because the studies on mirror neurons are still relatively new, I think the answers to those questions are still being determined. It does appear that people potentially have unequal amounts of mirror neurons in their craniums. This claim can be substantiated with some level of confidence due to the varying sizes of the different parts in our brains. That could be a factor in how we either naturally empathize or struggle in this area.

Another factor to consider is that we're talking about our brains performing a simulation. We observe someone faced with a dilemma and the mirror neurons in our brain process that stimulus as if we were encountering the same situation. We then notice their reaction, and those mirror neurons interpret their feelings or emotions based on the response. To me, the variables in this simulation are *observation* and *interpretation*. Some people are more observant than others and, therefore, performing more of these simulations in their own brains. And we interpret the responses of others through our own preconceptions and biases. So, if we see certain reactions or facial expressions, we tend to project what they mean for us.

How are we doing? Time to lighten the mood and stop with my scientist impersonation by saying that, as it turns out, being told you have mirror cells really is a compliment. I'll take any I can get. This R&D excursion was a long way of pointing out that our brains have been built to support empathizing. However, it still requires a dedicated effort. Some people need to work harder at empathy than others for reasons that require more investigating and explanation. And don't go away just yet; there's still more to say.

Empathy on Steroids

This is my clever way of describing something known as compassion. In essence, this feeling goes beyond the empathetic state of awareness in which we've delved. Compassion comes alive when being aware transcends into a motive for action. Do you remember when we discussed motives being the origin of motivation, which consequently drives our behaviors? They're important, to say the least. Those motives can pave the way for compassion, which is nothing more than a readiness to lend a helping hand. It represents a willing response to the needs of others. But what help do we offer? Here we find a hidden quandary that's more complicated than it appears at first glance.

At the root of this problem is the Golden Rule. This age-old guidepost is a principle that's meant to tell us how to model our lives. It states that we should treat others in the way we want to be treated. On a perfunctory level, it sounds like a noble pursuit. How could anyone argue that living by those words guarantees more empathy, and even compassion, in this world?

My inner contrarian just hit the buzzer. I have no idea how to spell the sound a buzzer makes and I gave it way too much thought. You'll just need to use your imagination. I believe the Golden Rule is egocentrism in disguise. Think about what it's literally telling us to do. We should treat people the way WE want to be treated. Why would we presume that another human being shares our same needs? How is it acceptable that we impose our standards and way of thinking on someone else? Sounds a little arrogant to me.

As a result, a different version of this principle has been put forth and is often touted as a better option. The Platinum Rule states that we should treat others the way *they* want to be treated, and I couldn't agree more with this premise. Did you hear that noise? That's the sound of a hammer hitting a nail squarely on its head. As much as I embrace the symbolism of platinum being a more valuable metal than gold, I'm not even sure a special name is needed for this rule because it exemplifies compassion. They're synonymous.

Don't confuse my accolades for compassion with suggesting it's required in all situations. That constitutes an unrealistic pipe dream. More importantly, it would be inauthentic. Compassion happens within us. It can't be forced or manufactured. But it also doesn't happen without empathy. That's the vital first step. More empathy begets more compassion. We achieve that revered understanding of the way others want to be treated by exercising awareness and listening skills, while remaining fully present in those moments. If we could only extend the same courtesy to ourselves. Or can we?

Self-Empathy

We've covered the importance of being more empathetic as we interact with others, which requires a diligent commitment to external awareness. But there's another type of empathy that's worth mentioning. And that's the empathy we impart toward ourselves. For that to happen, we need an internal alertness, also known as self-awareness.

This "know thyself" outlook can be characterized as a recognition and consciousness of our own feelings and emotions. We must establish this ongoing connection with ourselves. There's no argument about the fact that our mental state has a major impact on the actions and behaviors in which we decide to engage. Yes, I said "decide," because we have the freedom and power to choose them. A mindful awareness puts us in a position to make better choices.

Going a step further, self-awareness gives some insights into the empathy loop. If others are practicing empathy, they're aware of our feelings and emotions. By being aware of our own feelings and emotions, we're on the same page with others. They see what we see in ourselves and we can acknowledge their awareness. It's the "I know that you know and you know that I know" cycle.

On the flip side, self-awareness can often lead to self-judgment. We beat ourselves up. That could possibly be one of the reasons self-awareness is difficult for many people. Blocking it could be a defense mechanism people unconsciously activate as a way to prevent or avoid looking at themselves in the mirror.

If you hit me with that old standby, "What are you reading these days?" I would call out a name before you could finish the question. In my view, Mark Manson holds the top spot for most refreshing, astute author and thinker. He has created status-quo-challenging content on a wide range of topics that matter. Specifically, he has written about self-awareness, and his take on this concept really echoed within me. I have particularly found lasting value in a great connection he makes between the way self-awareness works with self-acceptance and how we view others. What a perfect fit for this discussion, right? A quote from his article *The Three Levels of Self-Awareness,* which rocked me, was, "Empathy can only occur in proportion to our own self-acceptance." Wow. I would fail epically in any feeble attempt to enhance that statement. Sometimes, but only sometimes, I know when to keep my mouth shut. This is one of those times.

I beseech you to work on practicing self-empathy and I commit, here and now, to continue doing a better job of taking my own advice. It will enhance your relationships with other people in addition to providing some necessary self-care. And please don't forget to give yourself a break.

My final, final thought on empathy is that it forges an opportunity for you to differentiate yourself. If you buy into my premise that empathy is rare, that means you have the ability to stand out from the crowd in a special way. Professional and personal contacts will view their interactions with you as unique and richer because, let's face it, that's how empathy rolls. It can also be an ally in your quest to climb into the rarified air of excellence in whatever you're aspiring to accomplish. Be different. Be excellent. Empathize.

Promises are rather multidimensional to me. They can be empty declarations for effect or sacred pacts. I offer both types but make an unfeigned effort to be stingy in making the latter, even more so when it comes to giving guarantees. So, these next statements equate to me going out on a limb.

Being more empathetic will make a positive impact on your Disruptive

Discovery efforts. Putting more empathy out there into the universe will make a positive impact on your life. Those are both promises. And I'm giving them lifetime guarantees.

24

THINGS I THINK

'll start with a preemptive apology.

I'm ultrasensitive to lecturing. I loathe having self-righteous sermons thrust in my direction. When people take a condescending tone and push *their* values that I should hold so dearly, whether in person or through another medium, I have a visceral reaction. While reading further, if you come to believe that I'm guilty of a double standard by displaying hypocrisy in violation of my own don't-go-there views on preachiness, have no hesitation in making a citizen's arrest and throw the book at me. And, under those circumstances, you won't hurt my feelings by skipping ahead to the next, and final, chapter. Just know that I'm racking my brain for a way to communicate what follows without such tenor. My intentions remain intact. I want to help you help people get to a better place. However, if at any point you determine that I've stepped out of my lane, please accept this cautionary mea culpa. Here goes nothing…

I have many thoughts, or so you've noticed. The people in my life would probably describe this collection of thinkings as profuse. That's a diplomatic way of rewording "here we go again" and "would you knock it off already?" In truth, I can't really blame them for these cries for help when I start expounding ideas. And do they ever suffer through me doing just that, unceasingly and often unsolicited.

Some of these thoughts clutter my head to the point they need to be released for fresh air. Others sound like the ravings of a madman as they leave my mouth, and I then desperately begin the futile act of trying to nullify any impending damage. Once in a blue moon, there's a conception worthy of shouting, "Eureka," if I do say so myself. These are the keepers I'd like to place in the limelight for you.

Before we storm the castle with the already mentioned final chapter, I wanted to take the time for a cleaning out of my mental and physical notebooks. This will be done by reflecting on several of the beliefs and ideas about which I'm passionate. You've allowed me to stand at the podium for this long. That's a privilege I won't abuse in relaying these thoughts to you. My commitment is to directly relate these bigger-picture philosophies in the context of Disruptive Discovery and the positive difference it can make in the lives of people. This romp through the woods will bring to light the musings either presently or at some point occupying space in my mind. These are the things I think. Or the things I think I think...I think.

⚡ Simpatico with discovery...

When we first started this rap session, I laid out the bedrock for discovery as a sweeping concept, its different definitions, and my interpretations. There was more to the story that wasn't disclosed at that time. It would have been too much, too soon. But this is an ideal opportunity to offer some additional inner feelings about discovery as an agent for movement. I figured now's as good a time as any because, let's face it, we're nearing the end of our road. While I still have your attention, it behooves me to put it all out there. This isn't a rehashing but, instead, a surge to leave everything on the field.

Constructing the model for Disruptive Discovery has been a long and grueling exercise. It has also been a fabulously rewarding campaign. Obscene amounts of raw materials and rough drafts have been stirring within my being for a period of time spanning multiple decades. When deciding I was all in and committed to giving this book thing a go, the work began on vigorously polishing the unfinished disciplines I'd been applying, reviewing, and adjusting. The vision was to create a user-friendly, intuitive process with real utilitarian implications that could be received and comprehended by others without needing a PhD. Intuition over intellect was constantly in the back of my mind so that authenticity could blossom.

In addition, this might come across as repeated minutiae, but words do matter and, therefore, more scrutiny than I care to admit was put into which term would be paired with "disruptive" for the title of this facilitation model. Discovery was a term to which I was exposed in the early stages of my career within the context of collaborating with customers and other professional associates to explore their needs. As I have adapted and refined my style over the years, discovery has remained the expression with which I have the most affinity.

When I started the process of putting pen to paper, or fingers to keys, I wondered if "discovery" was the right word to use with a new audience of readers. Would it resonate or click for newbies the way it did for me? Establishing that type of connection was crucial, so I performed some due diligence. Looking in a thesaurus, I found many synonyms, such as exploration, analysis, diagnosis, examination, and others. All of which are fantastic words and I always try to maintain a certain degree of vocabulary nimbleness. But I didn't feel a strong enough like-mindedness with any of them.

Through this consternation, my passion for uncovering that which is new made sure it was a round trip and brought me back to where I belonged. There was a laser pointer beaming on the term that's part of my fabric, with which I always enjoyed a harmonious relationship. Would it be out of line to play the soul mate card? Just don't tell my Wife…

Discovery.

That glorious word stands for going above and beyond passive curiosity. It's far stronger as a chase that only appeals to rare individuals. Happenings to discover can present themselves at any time and we pounce on them. There's no final destination because there's always more to uncover. The game can also change at any moment or evolve over time, so we adapt and keep going.

As I thought it through, the decision to partner "discovery" with "disruptive" was never really a decision at all. They fit together in that math-rule-defying utopia of the whole being more than the sum of its parts. And I will be their wingman anytime.

⚡ Mistakes are inevitable (or should be) and appreciated...

Do you want to get good at something? I don't mean just decent or respectable. Is there a talent you daydream about becoming world class, even GOAT-ish? Looking past yet another acronym, we can add this paradox to our collection... the best way to achieve excellence is by making mistakes and learning from them. It's the learning-from-them part of the statement that's priceless and indispensable.

Put yourself out there. Get uncomfortable. Take risks by trying some Disruptive Discovery concepts, especially any takeaways that reached out and put you in a headlock. Don't be afraid to ask a Question That Matters, even if you aren't certain about the timing or diction. If things go swimmingly, build on them. If you hit a bump in the road, learn from the mistakes, apply what was learned, and keep punching. Any miscalculations or setbacks don't reflect incompetence. In fact, I can't imagine achieving competence in any area by clinging to safety and not testing the waters out of fear of missteps.

Getting your nose bloodied doesn't sound pleasant, but I highly recommend placing yourself in positions from which you'll be knocked down, assuming those lumps are the unfortunate result of positive intentions and responsible actions. There aren't many more admirable ways to improve in just about anything that's difficult than making mistakes or, at a minimum, pushing outside the confines of self-preservation to a place in which they're possible, if not anticipated. Skydiving, juggling chainsaws, and alligator wrestling are obvious exceptions.

⚡ Beware the learning snobs...

Disruptive Discovery can fire on all cylinders when used to solve a challenging problem or to improve in a development area. You've been there, done that, got the souvenir. When it comes to discovery, as a whole, there are no limitations to when, where, or how it can come about. Discovery is all about uncovering new things. Yes, I know, you have a hat from that vacation too.

When finding out something novel or unfamiliar, we expand our learning. This can go down anywhere and everywhere. There are some who have strong viewpoints about the right way to learn. They feel there's a proper manner in which to gain knowledge. They know who they are. Some methods are placed high on a pedestal and others frowned upon as being lowbrow. I say ignore them, and don't feel guilted or pressured into thinking there's a certain, right way to expose your mind to new teachings. Seek out learning situations that work best for you and avoid letting spontaneous education pass you by.

Our dissection of learning began right out of the gate and has been a running theme ever since. Not only is learning pivotal for our growth and development, it's a necessity for survival. I might be speaking to the choir because the fact that you chose a book with this title says you know what's what. Different types of learning situations have already been noted, but I wanted to reframe them, perhaps with a unique spin. Because I can only advocate for myself, I'll make sure to speak in the first person for this retrospection...

Just about all I've learned went down in one of two distinct ways.

First, I should address learning in an active form. This mode of collecting information is what I would consider experiential or firsthand. A short list of primary examples that come to mind include hands-on training, attempting something for the first time, group activities, conversations with other people, and more traditional courses, conferences, seminars, or online learning platforms. For me, observation is an active adaptation of learning because of mirror neurons and the scientific gobbledygook I rhapsodized about not long ago. Simply put, I learn tons by witnessing the behavior of others. A case could also be made for reading because I sometimes find that to be an active form of learning, depending on the extent of my engagement and my capacity to process the material.

The second route from which I continuously reap the benefits of stimulating discoveries shows itself in more passive formats. This type of learning takes place as a one-way transfer of information, pushed or fed through a particular means. Some of the aforementioned training, conferences, seminars, and online learning aptly fit this description, when the agenda or activities are structured with less interaction.

It's controversy time. Do you want to know another source of so many life lessons for me? Watching TV. Yes, you heard me. Watching TV. The small screen. The tube. The idiot box.

Usually about five seconds after making such a claim is right around the time people feel obligated to educate me on reading being so superior to watching mindless drivel on TV or any other electronic device. I typically save those people the time and concede what I already know. The research and studies performed don't bode well for us binge-watchers of favorite shows when compared to the benefits of reading. I'm not falling on that sword or charging that hill.

Reading is obviously an important skill. Children and adults must be able to read to thrive in this world. I'm not a moron or a caveman, depending on who you ask. And I attribute so much of who I am, and who I am still trying to become, as a person to reading. It's mostly a passive learning form in my experience because of a lack of emotional connection and engagement with the material. Of course, that statement teeters on the blasphemous without pointing out that it comes with an enormous asterisk. There is an impressive collection of publications and authors to which I attribute acutely positive changes in my life. Several of them have been referenced and I will suggest others later. However, in general, new perspectives I gain through reading are realized through volumes of quantity, not necessarily quality.

Books are great. Whether they're fiction, nonfiction, self-help, motivational, or any other genre from the long list of choices. I don't read enough books, but, when I do, incremental positive changes are typically the result. And we can't forget about articles, blogs, and even social media as reading options. They're great vehicles for getting access to ideas that have been researched, a range of perspectives, facts, opinions, opinions, opinions, and even an opinion or two. Vetting your sources is obviously the key to absorbing information from these platforms.

Back to my stumping for TV—I'm sticking to my guns. Throughout my life, I've learned a copious number of lessons from watching series after series, movies, documentaries, sporting events, specials, and even game shows. For a cherry on top, so many family memories and bonding moments have been scored during our group TV sessions.

Depending on how you feel about dopamine, because apparently our brains produce it when we go into binge mode, the pleasure we sense when watching TV might or might not have advantages. But I think we can agree that it gives us a little feel-good something and our brains enjoy the ride. Fly in the ointment? There's nothing to see here.

To continue, people somehow justify spending overwhelming amounts of time "buried in a good book." But if you confess to spending twenty hours over the weekend ripping through every season of a new must-watch series a colleague recommended, they might silently judge your choice as a frivolous, or unhealthy, waste of time.

Bullshit.

Such a strong objection calls for a qualifier. I'm not suggesting those twenty hours glued to whatever streaming service were intended for self-betterment or picking up a few IQ points. But entertainment, in any shape or size, is another form of experience that can lead to learnings equally valuable compared to those gained through more scholarly activities. At least that's what my TV-biased, jedi-mind-tricked head believes.

Reading stimulates the brain. Watching screens also stimulates the brain. They both simulate experiences in our minds. There is valuable stuff going on in there and maintaining permanent residency, or squatter rights. That's how we learn! I'll cop to my defensive, The Other Side persona doing most of this talking. And my contrarianism is probably on overdrive, albeit well-intentioned, as always. But I'm confident we can settle on maintaining some semblance of balance being what really counts. Even if it's the kind of balance that looks like eating a side of broccoli to wash down a massive plate of nachos and stuffed crust pizza to rationalize eating a healthy dinner.

I've been talking a lot about me and my learning experiences. I chose this first-person approach to reinforce the point that I strongly encourage you to do what works for *you*. Please steer clear of trying to force a learning approach based on feelings of guilt, pressure, or insecurity about what other people say, do, or imply. The upshot is that all of us have been given an incredible gift in the ability to learn. If there's new knowledge to be gained, grab it, regardless of the source. Don't miss out by being snooty over style points. Never stop expanding your bandwidth. Be a learning enthusiast. And don't you dare ever feel ashamed about a life lesson you picked up from a sitcom.

⚡ Marketers could learn a thing or two...

The bulk of our attention has been geared toward individuals and groups. However, there are implications in other spheres worthy of mention. Disruptive Discovery can have ramifications at an organizational level, including companies and other entities such as departments, committees, clubs, and the list goes on. Speaking of departments, I don't want to pick on marketing. Oops, that was disingenuous. You busted me in a bald-faced lie. My nose just grew a smidgeon. I *do* want to pick on marketing.

In my day job, I frequently witness an epidemic of misguided positioning statements by companies touting themselves through brochures, e-marketing, and numerous sorts of promotional activities. At home, I pay close attention to commercials during those rare instances of watching TV (funny, right?) and also notice various advertisements when out and about. What I routinely behold is a chronic syndrome that has stricken so many marketers. More times than not, these companies work diligently to push the *features* of whatever product or service they're trying to sell. Diligent, but nevertheless misguided.

Notice the terminology I selected...*features*. There's a canyon-sized difference between *features* and *benefits*. Most companies are oblivious to this mammoth dissimilarity, but we can table that thought for another day. At any rate, this clubbing people over the head with features is the strategy marketing folks exploit to convince customers that they'll be a pariah if they don't buy whatever's being sold. Unbeknownst to them, most consumers are deaf, numb, or desensitized to this type of plugging. Why? Great question. And one that matters, by the way.

The underlying reason I'm able to make this claim is because companies far too often push features THEY think are important, not necessarily as a response to addressing the needs of their customers. Put another way, just because a product or service does something (feature) doesn't mean that something solves a problem (benefit). As a result, there's a gentle whisper coming from buyers in reply to those pitches. If you listen closely, you can hear what they're saying.

"*So what?*"

Yessir! Another cameo from a Question That Matters, but not the reaction you want to hear from consumers. Marketers can avoid this kiss of death by inviting the Disruptive Discovery model into their research and analysis. There are ways to creatively apply this method on a broader scale, but nothing beats hearing directly from the people purchasing products or services. Either way, it will quickly reveal an unavoidable reality of marketing…people buy things for their own reasons, not ours.

⚡ Disruptive Discovery can also take place from within...

This process is most often used as a facilitation in extraneous situations. We've mapped it out as an approach focusing outside ourselves. But what I'm about to give away is like a goody bag filled with beautifully sublime yet unintended consequences that you've picked up without even knowing. Consider it a party favor.

By learning how to administer this method in an outward manner, you've also given yourself a change instrument that can be used for inward "me projects." There's tremendous value in the Disruptive Discovery process when used within ourselves. Nothing changes with the model. The only departure is you assuming the role of both Facilitator and participant. In effect, you're communicating with yourself, but not in the way that gets the neighbors talking. This is inner dialogue for well-being. You have access to all the skills we've been studying together that are now a work in progress, including trust building and listening.

This practice can get you to better places. I do it on a regular basis. I mean personal Disruptive Discovery, not talking to myself (I prefer sending texts to my own phone and then thinking of witty responses). Putting that aside aside, this is an exercise in which you ask yourself the prescribed questions, give yourself honest answers, listen to yourself, and continue taking *you* through the process. This could resemble self-guided therapy, or maybe a more complex form of meditation. Either way, go for it. My hunch is that, if carried out properly, you'll find the challenges that exist when facilitating with others are the same as those you face when discovering within yourself, perhaps even more prominent.

There might be a development area you want to tackle and improve. Maybe you're considering a significant change in your career or personal life. There could be a daunting decision keeping you up at night. Or what about that problem gnawing at you because of the unshakable gut feeling of an enhanced solution sitting out there, waiting? What if previously unexplored options could emerge in a status-quo-shattering way? Funny you should ask.

⚡ Original ideas are scarce...

And they're becoming scarcer.

There's so much information floating around out there and, for my two cents, that makes it far too easy for people to recycle ideas from other sources versus stimulating their own thoughts. Why is that a problem? Because it handicaps our ability to broaden perspectives. We get trapped in the boxes of what's spoon-fed to us instead of making a concerted effort to think differently, challenge preexisting positions, and give rise to pure, needle-moving ideas. There's a convenience factor in taking what we're told at face value, agreeing or disagreeing, and then either promoting or attacking, depending on the fit with our already firmly established viewpoints. No, thank you, not interested. I'd rather eat a plate of glass and wash it down with a tall cup of bleach.

If I've said it once, I've said it a thousand times, and I'll keep on shouting it from the rooftops...Disruptive Discovery can change the game. It can make a difference. I believe those pronouncements with everything I have. The process can open minds and take us to the promised land of freethinking. And that, my fellow disruptors, is a liberating and empowering ability worth repeating.

Freethinking.

This distinguished class of an entitlement (the good kind) is vastly underused. I propose we change that unfortunate reality starting right here, right now. We should pledge to become more dedicated and active freethinkers. And let's commit to allowing Disruptive Discovery to do its thing by encouraging others to find the freethinker that resides inside themselves. Maybe we can institute a Declaration of Independence 2.0 to include a fourth unalienable right...

Life, Liberty, the Pursuit of Happiness, and Freethinking.

By skimming the Disruptive Discovery model and 10 Questions That Matter, you'll see several components that jump off the page as catalysts for freethinking and original idea generation:

- Establishing a Mutual Concern mindset defies predisposed tendencies for us to either protect what is mine or give what is yours. Greatness can arise from this unnatural effort to convene around what's ours together.

- Listening skills bring about understanding of what others are saying and not stopping short with the physiological act of hearing.

- QTMs fit the bill. Most notably, we know that "What if?" "So what?" and The Other Side questions almost flagrantly pry open mentalities that might otherwise remain closed. Without open-mindedness, a precondition to freethinking, those questions crash into a brick wall. But this entire collection of questions breaks through the surface by contemplating that which matters. Such contemplation, by definition, requires deeper thinking.

From here, things get real. The original ideas that result from freethinking translate into diversity of thought. Now we're cooking with gas. Diversity of thought has never been more urgent in our society and will never again be this insignificant. Chew on that mindbender for a minute.

Anything that injects more diversity of thought into our mental atmosphere should be hailed, and we can play a role as change ambassadors through Disruptive Discovery. I should also mention that freethinking has a cousin. Allow me to make the introduction.

⚡ We need more critical thinking...

The use of "critical" to brand thought patterns can be misleading. It often carries a negative connotation, and that's an unfortunate misinterpretation. Critical thinking can be a progressive activity and, in many cases, a much-needed exercise. Conjecture? Perhaps. But I'll do my darnedest to offer up sufficient evidence with minimal meandering. We should start with an explanation of what critical thinking is *not*:

- It is *not* pessimism, a proclivity to see in a negative light.
- It is *not* cynicism, a tendency toward distrusting the motives of others.
- It is *not* contrarianism, a disposition to adopt opposing viewpoints (know anyone with that trait?).
- It is *not* realism, an inclination to see things as they are.
- And it is *not* even criticism, an expression of disapproval.

Critical thinking is when we form our own beliefs, opinions, and judgments. It's an analysis performed through the amalgamation of facts, observations, interactions, and other experiences. This is how we develop character. This is how convictions are formed. These are the goods in which integrity is founded. For anyone aspiring to make a positive difference, consider them must-have attributes. I wish this complete catalog for my Daughters, if that says anything.

The mere suggestion I'm making is that we view critical thinking in those terms and don't allow it to be found guilty by misunderstood association with the other named forms of reasoning. We should ache for more critical thinking in our daily activities and relationships, both personally and professionally. Arguing against this need stresses me out and gives me a rash (I'm really laying it on thick), so just know that my fingers are crossed in hopes that such a temptation doesn't cross your mind. As I've barked with my megaphone on multiple occasions, our intentions rule the day. With the proper intention, critical thinking *does not* equal criticism.

⚡ I now understand the reason compromise is such a struggle for some people....

When reviewing The Other Side as a QTM, we briefly referenced compromise. If I remember correctly, someone who'll remain nameless profoundly stated that our diminishing ability to find common ground is putting the art of compromise on the brink of extinction. He further preachified that it was already an endangered species. High and mighty sounding or not, those positions contain much truth. There's more to be said, granted sometimes less *is* more, so I'll stick with that plan of attack.

This could initially strike you as neurosis over semantics, but there's an important difference between the middle ground and common ground. We find the *middle* ground by identifying differences in positions and splitting them, hence the phrase, "split the difference." We land on *common* ground by finding interests that are shared and centering around those bounties.

I've often been told that you know when a negotiation is successful when all parties involved feel pain. Maybe there's some merit in that depressing rule of thumb. But what if I retorted with a so-crazy-it-just-might-work idea of building on what we have in common, our Mutual Concerns, as opposed to making sure enough jelly beans are given away from each pile so we can feel justified saying that everyone lost something?

The problem with the middle ground is that it becomes a zero-sum game. For one person to get what they want, the other person needs to give up something they want, and vice versa. Compromise should be about magnifying our similarities instead of prioritizing and exacerbating our differences. To further outline the inherent quagmire of this easier-said-than-done idealism, our natural tendency is to protect what's ours. That means we're going against human nature in a battle that's tough to win. The more we default to this tendency, the more a muscle memory type reaction takes control.

I acknowledge the dilemma we face with fighting back, but I refuse to stay down for the count. Fortunately, several of the techniques in Disruptive Discovery make it manageable and realistic to compromise more effectively. Listening skills, empathy, Mutual Concern, and several of the Questions That Matter can do the trick winningly. They can lead to compromise looking less like what's being given up and more like what's being gained for all stakeholders.

⚡ I do wonder what our planet would say...

If Mother Earth could talk, I would give anything to be a Facilitator and take her through the most awe-inspiring of Disruptive Discovery exercises. Many would contend that she does possess a voice and converses in her own language. Can you imagine asking our planet these Questions That Matter:

What do you like most about us? And what's your least favorite thing that we do?

You've been to a few rodeos over the past four and a half billion years or so, why do you think human beings treat one another the way they do?

To continue along with this "Quick, find a straitjacket for Geoff" escapade, I wonder what we would learn about how the earth perceives the Opening that exists between its Current and Aspirational States. We've only been walking this planet for a blip on the screen, relatively speaking. And depending on the answers to those high-stakes questions, we might be on a path to disruptively discover responses we would rather not understand. We could begin to uncover ramifications that do far more than matter.

I'm not making political commentary. That's not my bag and, for me, politics are perhaps the least favorite part of every day. Again, no, thanks. My hands are full enough. As I'm still trying to ease into this gig of the amateur philosopher and take it all in, I simply figured why not take a stab at applying the key concepts of this book to the big picture by thinking out of this world, pun intended.

Would you look at the time? It's probably wise for me to stop before I get myself into trouble. In the words of Forrest Gump, "That's all I have to say about that."

But I am curious.

25

NOW WHAT?

Could there be a better way to start our last chapter together than with a heaping scoop of cynicism? I agree. Sounds peachy keen to me too. Into the darkness we go. After you...

When last discussing the nonmechanical yet process driven structure of our model—that seems like an eternity ago—we were settling on a Disruptive Discovery Understanding. Picking up where we left off, the formulation of that accord supplies us with a strong base going forward. Once you sense satisfactory desire is present with all participants, combined with a befitting amount of buy-in about expectations, it's time to get busy.

We have reached a stage where acting is becoming increasingly arduous for anyone trying to fake it. This point in time is a zero hour marking the last chance for stakeholders to speak now or forever hold their peace. We are ready to perform a litmus test by asking the most revealing, card-showing of questions. It's imperative that we know if they are ready.

TIME-OUT...

Hold that thought because there are a few things I need to get off my chest. I somehow swore an oath to tell it like it is, so hang on to your hat for a round of realism-cynicism hybrid views. Posing a readiness indicator is fertile ground for pushback. To find yourself standing at this place, many obstacles have undoubtedly been overcome. A job well done and I'm giving you mental high-fives, fist bumps, or one of those celebratory athlete hugs. Brace yourself as we come to grips with a few nasty obstacles that remain:

- People make excuses
- People lie

Which one should we bum out over first? Rock-paper-scissors…

People Make Excuses

A large number of popular objections or concerns roll off the tongue when people are nudged out of a comfort zone. Individuals could express fear or reluctance. They might feel the task at hand is too difficult or overwhelming. Maybe there's an anticipation of resistance from higher-ups, coworkers, family, friends, or others if they continue down a particular path. In many cases, these are legitimate concerns. But you're more than ready for them, whether you know it or not. More than likely, during the Disruptive Discovery process, you'll have uncovered enough insight to help overcome that pushback. This is a great time for you to be supportive and talk them down from the ledge.

Then, there's the other species of stall tactics, and those aren't so easily overcome. There are lots of different names for such cop-outs, but I say we call them like we see them and refer to them as what they are: excuses.

People keep a plethora of them at the ready and, if none of those shoes fit a pending avoidance situation, they're adroit at thinking on their feet and breaking out an unworn pair from the box in a split second. Excuses come fast and furious. There are too many to cover, but there's a particular brand of shirking sneakers that deserves some barbing. One of the most common you'll hear is, "I don't have enough time." How often do we hear that there aren't enough hours in the day?

Bullshit.

I know I just hit you with one of these profanity indulgences not long ago and my spacing needs some work, but this was warranted. Plus, that was number four. I reached my "do not exceed" quota. Hope you had as much fun finding BS Easter eggs as I had hiding them.

I've come to realize there are, in reality, plenty of hours in the day. On the days in which my wakey-wakey time is three a.m. instead of four a.m., I sometimes feel like there are *too many* hours! People use that thinking and widely accepted fact of life as an excuse, in my opinion. It becomes a convenient way to enable procrastination. After all, I would put the actual number of hours in a day at the top of the list for things that are completely out of our control. It's right up there with the sun rising in the morning, when the elevator will arrive even though we keep pushing the button, and how many Peanut M&M's we eat in one sitting. The hours in each day are constant, predictable resources. There are twenty-four of them in sixty-minute installments, no exceptions (other than the whole daylight savings fiasco). We all share the onus of using them wisely.

The cold truth is that people invest effort and energy into what they value. If something is all-important for us, we find the time. Period. It's that simple. Therefore, this becomes a conversation about priorities, not time. Let's keep it real. There are usually enough hours in the day for the things we deem pressing, if we're being honest with ourselves.

People say, "I'm so busy." To that, I say, "Get over it." Everyone is busy. Now that I'm stepping into crossing-the-line territory, I should also mention such a statement can be insulting. If someone is telling me why they haven't responded to a request or answered an e-mail by saying, "I've been so busy," what they're really saying is, "I've been so busy *doing things that are more important to me than whatever you are asking for.*" This extended version is completely fine with me. I personally respect and appreciate honesty over excuses. I mean, how long does it realistically take to respond to an e-mail? Maybe forty-five seconds? OK, I'll cede five minutes. That's 300 seconds. There are still 86,100 left in that day. Want to subtract eight hours of sleep and ten more hours of dedicated work and family time in which there's absolutely no way multitasking could possibly take place? I'll further concede with no skin off my back. There are still 21,300 seconds available in a day. Get the picture?

Those mini-tirades are exhausting. You could have stopped me, or at least pretended you weren't listening.

Hello.

Heeeellllllllloooo?!

Want another cheery thought to really brighten your day? How about this one....

People Lie

We do. Whether it's nature, nurture, Adam, or Eve, I'm not bright enough to offer a rationalization for our penchant to toss lies around like candy. But we fib, fabricate, deceive, exaggerate, cheat, misinform, and butcher the truth with alarming ease. My reason for stating this undeniable ABC of life isn't to disappoint or discourage you. It's simply another factor we must acknowledge, and even celebrate, in our efforts to interact with other people.

They tell us things we want to hear in an attempt to appease or placate. They embellish, which is a form of lying. They make promises and commitments with no plan to honor them so we'll leave them alone. They cling to their own version of reality to avoid pain and consequences. Some find satisfaction in the challenge of seeing what they can get away with saying. They lie, plain and simple. In the moment, it could seem less troublesome than rolling with honesty. Not telling the truth might also be an escape plan for avoiding feelings of disapproval, rejection, or other unpleasantries.

Unfortunately, this presents a challenge in keeping things moving along at this stage of Disruptive Discovery. We can be lulled into thinking that continued forward progress is imminent. Talk is cheap in some situations and intentionally misleading in others. The irony is that truth in those conversations—the real truth—could very well be that there is a more realistic chance of someone getting where they're trying to go by dealing with adversity instead of pretending everything is hunky-dory.

What do we do with this rain I just poured on our parade? We keep marching and don't empower that thunderstorm to ruin anything. We control what we can control, eyes laser-focused on the ball. So, now what?

With the nonstop alibis, especially about insufficient time, and the reality that people luxuriate in falsehoods, you would think there's no hope, right? But that's not the case. Not by a long shot. I learned a long time ago that the best defense is a good offense. We can take what we know about human nature, the proclivity for excuse making and lie telling, and use it to our advantage. Sometimes bluffs need to get called, and if that works, a jolt of energy is added to the process. And that brings us back to where I was trying to go before that uplifting journey through the land of excuses and lies.

TIME-IN....

We were in the midst of summarizing what was learned in the Disruptive Discovery process. Along with the accompaniment of a passable desire level and a thumbs-up about expectations, this serves as our Disruptive Discovery Understanding. Next up, all players should begin formulating ideas about what they're going to do with the agreement that's now firmly in place. Otherwise, we venture into if-a-tree-falls-in-the-forest territory, and that's a no-no.

Energy should smoothly redistribute into planning for what happens next, as formally or informally as necessary, depending on the situation. In a nutshell, such a plan is nothing more than the specific activities to follow. It's a charge to do something, to take action. No need to show fancy diagrams or those figures I know you like so much. A plan can range from a highly intricate document to doodle on a bar napkin. We'll take whatever gets the job done. At this stage, it would be wise to reinforce that ownership for this course of action belongs to them. It's being crafted based on their responses and desires, not ours. There's no need to do us any favors and our only skin in the game is the time invested, along with a keenness for them to arrive at the better place we are trying to reach together.

This isn't to say that we're passing the buck or skirting responsibility. We're by their side as a support resource. Such backing reassures participants to find their moxie as they recalibrate from "want to" into action. Even though this is *their* plan to achieve success in *their* betterment project, we want to assist. In this regard, little things go a long way as we shift into this mode:

- Reinforce the path that has been chosen and any gains or improvements at stake upon arrival.

- Their dedication to seeing the process through is admirable and it takes guts, whether the application is personal or professional. There's absolutely nothing wrong with saying so.

- People often take comfort in knowing we have their back and will remain present. Concerns, objections, and excuses could keep popping up, just like playing Whack-A-Mole. Keep addressing them as they rear their cute but cunning little heads.

- Arranging for ongoing check-ins, wanting to know what you can do for them, can add to well-being and contentment.

For the grand finale, there's one remaining question that must be put on the table. Once everyone involved is dialed into the plan going forward, this will determine whether to hit the launch button or if more time is needed in a particular area, or multiple elements, of the model. Transition questions move us from Surface Discovery into Disruptive Discovery. What I'm about to lay before you is meant to swiftly move us from Disruptive Discovery into kinetics. In plain English, the time has come for getting this show on the road. I'll advise a technique meant to jump-start implementation, execution, and forward movement. It reflects a much more polite and sensitive version of "put up or shut up." This looming question might sound familiar because of the little dance performed around it not long ago. It was a bid at giving a peekaboo preview as further auditioning off my cutting edge, avant-garde writing style.

Are you ready?

That was klutzy of me. See, I'm still a novice. And a fledgling one at that. Sorry for the mix-up. I'm not asking if you're ready for me to reveal the question. That *is* the question you should ask participants at this stage:

Are you ready?

A pseudo-Question That Matters #11 to aid in the passage from discoveries that really matter into the motivation that really matters. It was a contender for making the guest list to our QTM shindig, but quite possibly would have sent regrets. Standing on its own two feet, we're looking at a question needing no invitation to other events. This call to action with a question mark has a very precise and clear mission. We should give action its due as a zealot, and what better way than with a motif? I'm sensing one in our future and there's no time like the present.

By posing "Are you ready?" this action-based inquiry becomes an action-based challenge. One that is accepted merely by getting started somewhere, anywhere. Or by doing something, anything. I'm a believer that success begets success. With a modification to that prophecy, I also stand firm in another theorem.

Action begets more action.

Way back when, like way, way back when, somebody was hungry. Not just hungry but flirting-with-starvation hungry, because they looked at an elephant and started making a plan for eating them. They were thinking big. A midday snack wasn't going to satisfy their growling tummy. The goal was to devour the whole elephant, and they determined this could only happen one bite at a time. As purposeless as this cockamamie story may sound, there's relevance we can leverage at this juncture.

If you're giving me a sideways look from the elephant talk, it's warranted. How about another angle? I'm not good with my hands, and that's being generous. But I'm pretty sure houses only get built brick by brick. If your digs are being constructed from wood, siding, or stucco, the same principle applies. How many home-building materials are there anyway? I left out hay, but I think that fell out of favor after the whole incident with those three pigs and the wolf (wood too, for that matter). Regardless, the idea is that we accomplish endeavors potentially overwhelming in scope bit by bit.

We can build on methodical increments, and eventually the end product begins to take shape. In some cases, growth and change can occur more exponentially than incrementally. None of which happens without that first step. Even with a ready-FIRE-aim undertone, that first step—any step—can be more like a long jump. Think back to when we were kicking around the idea of not letting perfect become the enemy of good enough. This might be a ~~perfect~~ good enough time for cozying up to that common-sensical way of getting things done.

You can be a mobility champion by promoting such a positive prejudice and bias toward action. Plus, any Facilitator watching their Disruptive Discovery efforts spring to life is a hyperfruitful experience, and then some. And every championship deserves a parade down Broad Street. Did you think I would forget coming back to that reference? It was a subliminal, secret handshake message to Philadelphia sports fans. If this notice about my allegiance is too late, I can only ask for forgiveness.

Quickly changing subjects, do you have a minute? There's something weighing heavy on my mind and it involves someone you know. I wanted to pick your brain about this person.

You.

This comes with a caveat. I've been doing my best to create manageable expectations and thwart any temptation to overpromise how much your life is going to change at the conclusion of this affair. But I do think there's some value in the mushy-motivational, self-helpish advice I'm about to bestow. If at any point you feel the urge to disappointedly sigh and murmur under your breath, "What a sellout. I can't believe he went there," don't forget the sincerity of my intentions or the WHY that brought us here in the first place.

On any given day, there's a constantly revolving carousel of exposures we see and hear. Those contact points can offer brand-spanking-new information, perspectives, learnings, answers, and so many other takeaways with varying ranges of novelty. But how often do they stimulate action, change hearts and minds, or transform behavior?

Usually, it's the compelling events and activities that drive those changes. And for something to reach compelling status means different things for different people. You probably have the impression I have an ax to grind with most training programs, seminars, books, and other tools designed to improve skills. More likely, I'm merely coming across as a nag. These are points that have validity, but I'm holding my ground. All those resources, and many others, are frequently loaded with thought-out content leading to note-scribbling and swearings of, "I'm absolutely going to start doing that!" But somewhere down the road, such resolutions lose their steam. For some reason, the renaissance and turning-over-a-new-leaf moments fizzle with nothing, or not much, eventuating. They don't become inflection points and, therefore, were clearly never compelling events in the first place.

I'm getting down on my knees for this closing monologue...

If Disruptive Discovery falls prey to the same destiny for you, I would be crushed, heartbroken, devastated, or some other overly dramatic emotion. So, I have a suggestion to prevent this tragedy from happening. I believe the missing ingredient for all those outlets missing the mark is a call to action. With that being said, I now have a final question, and it might ultimately be the only one that really matters:

Are YOU *ready?*

No, this isn't déjà vu. And I'm aware I previously recommended asking this exact question to participants as a means to stimulate next steps. But take notice of the strategically capitalized Y-O-U. Yes, we use this question to propel everyone involved in the process into action. But it also applies right here, right now. That question is the call to action for *you*. It's my way of looking you in the eye, with my knees now beginning to throb, and asking if you'll commit to start using Disruptive Discovery in the different roles you play in your personal and professional worlds. At the end of the day, or the end of this book, our conversation needs to center around where you go from here. It's about either embracing these learnings and putting them to work or placing them on the shelf to sit with all the other nice-but-no-dice experiences. That's the question. So…are you ready?

If so, let 'er rip. I don't have much to say beyond what has already been said, and I've said a lot! There are people out there waiting for you to make a positive difference in their lives. They're thanking you in advance but just don't know it yet.

If you aren't ready, I encourage further exploration to uncover what's holding you back. Quite possibly there's confusion about specific components of the model or even more holistic apprehension. I'm also enough of a big boy to handle any skepticism or lack of confidence that this method will produce results. Whatever the case, I implore you to diagnose the source of your hesitation. Either go back and reassess those areas to become comfortable or contact me for clarification. That's not an empty offer, and I'd look forward to those interactions. But please, please don't let this time you've invested be thrown on the pile with other casualties of waste.

Disruptive Discovery works. This facilitation model can make a meaningful impact. And you, as a Facilitator of Betterment, are capable of using it in helping people get to a better place. I hope this has been a compelling event for you—so much so that you are now bursting at the seams to go get disruptive!

I'm a strong believer in the idea that, if you have something meaningful to say and feel the message can be a difference-maker, you should say it. Well, there were clearly a few things on my mind. And, as the reality hits that I'm now typing the last words of everything I felt worthy of being said, tears are forming in my eyes. This has been an incredible experience for me.

My own personal Disruptive Discovery is a process I continue to facilitate and don't ever plan to stop. When minibreakthroughs occur, those steps toward a better place carry an awesome sense of self-enlightenment. Consequently, recognizing the significance of gratitude in our well-being is a quality I find myself more aware of than ever. After all, I declared gratitude as the fifth most powerful force in the universe. I try to practice it every day. Being grateful is another one of those muscles in our psyche.

You've entrusted me with much of your time, energy, and attention. Thank you for reading and sharing those precious belongings. You've made an investment I hold sacred. I'm so grateful and incredibly honored.

In the words of Rocky Balboa after he beat Apollo Creed for the Heavyweight title, "Except for my kid being born, this is the greatest night in the history of my life!" The Italian Stallion had a way with words, didn't he? This was right after he said, "I love yous too," for added effect. I intensely relate to his goose-bump-inducing announcement, although it isn't a complete parallel for my situation. First, I have two Daughters, so this proclamation would need to be pluralized. Next, my Wife miraculously altering the course of my life by agreeing to spend the rest of hers with me was, you know, a big deal. And there have been a few other noteworthy moments scattered over the years. Not to mention the fact that it's 4:28 a.m., throwing a monkey wrench into the whole night ambience. Suffice it to say, I know where Rocky was heading in his own style, and this moment feels pretty amazing.

I gotta go. Time to lace up the shoes and sneak in a disgustingly early run while listening to my favorite Neil Diamond playlist. Or maybe I should get a jump on the day and hit 'em with the Hein! Oh, wait! Am I behind on *Grey's Anatomy* and duty bound to catch up on an episode? Let's not forget about all the floors out there needing to be cleaned. There's so much to do. Looks like I should reconsider getting on TikTok to help with my time management. I'm sort of hungry, so an early morning breakfast could be the answer. I wish we had a pie in the fridge. But only if it's my favorite kind...

ACKNOWLEDGMENTS

still can't believe that just happened. I'm in awe that this little writing project is complete. For so long, I figured pure delusion had seeped into my brain when I told myself I might have a book in me. Who would have thunk that all the nonsense filling my head could become a work capable of a fate beyond aimlessly bumping around in there forever. I was resigning myself to the increasingly evident certainty that it was nothing more than jibberish. If I'm being honest, that's exactly what would have happened if not for a few people who have had a far-reaching influence on me.

During my life, I have been fortunate, blessed, charmed, and downright lucky to have crossed paths with a long list of incredible people. Among that group are several extraordinarily special individuals to whom I owe a debt I will struggle to ever fully repay. You see, without these people, this book would never have become a reality. A few I consider friends, a few are new connections, a few I haven't yet had the privilege to meet, and one is sadly no longer with us. In their own unique ways, each of those individuals played an integral role in generously giving me everything I needed to turn a dream into a reality (even if they gave it unknowingly!). The gratitude I feel toward each person is more than I can describe (even if I am about to describe it anyway). I can only hope for an opportunity to return the favor. Maybe I should send a gift basket with a balloon bouquet. I'll work on that. Until it arrives at their door, this is the best way I know to say, "Thank you."

Simon Sinek helped me to discover and incarnate my WHY. Reading *Start with Why* precipitated a poor man's vision quest to understand my greater purpose and gave me a new lens through which to see so many situations. His TED Talk is a must see. If you haven't already done so, the video is very easy to find and I'm unafraid to vow it will open your eyes.

The Golden Circle is a theory he explains, and I believe every organization should give it serious consideration. To go a step further, perhaps many steps, I believe this model has a place for teams, departments, groups, and individuals. I was immediately taken in by The Golden Circle, and easily found the motivation necessary for creating my own.

After reading *Find Your Why*, a book that offers a walk-through of several templates, I was able to fine-tune my personal Golden Circle, and it has become a tremendous guide for me. There is a deep-rooted connection with my personal and professional activities every day. Disruptive Discovery is a big part of my WHY, and I hope this movement started by Simon Sinek continues to grow.

Mark Manson helped me find my voice. I mentioned this author in the book's text, but I can't overhype the positive changes I embarked on after reading *The Subtle Art of Not Giving a F*ck*. That book rocked me, and I've been a fanboy ever since. I devour his writing like it's going out of style and can barely keep up with his newsletters, articles, and so much other content. Through all that consumption, I've felt challenged to rethink the manner in which I view human behavior and process my values. Because of his The "Do Something" Principle, I actually started taking all my notes and putting them into book form.

I was oblivious to the idea that writing could be done with such a conversational style. Thankfully, this *can* be done and nobody is better at doing it than Mark Manson, bar none. I've learned so much from his thinking ever since getting maybe halfway through the first page, more like the first paragraph.

A practical resource for developing my own enlightenment had been much needed. He has no idea, but his writing has been such a vehicle. Without this outlet, I have a hunch my ideas, theories, and observations would still be collecting dust. He encourages readers to send e-mails with no promises beyond they will be read, so I sent him a message when waffling about writing a book. He responded in his own authentic way suggesting to write the book first and see what I think about it. After reading enough of his publications, I knew exactly what he was saying. It was a gracious reply, but I could almost hear him telling me to quit whining, write the damn thing, and then figure it out. So, I did. That was a perfect push and an important factor during the self-doubt phases of this project, when endurance was everything.

You know that hypothetical question people kick around sometimes, "If you could have a beer with someone, who would it be?" I think Mark Manson would be my choice. Buying him a drink and saying, "Thanks, dude!" would be the least I could do as repayment. Assuming, of course, he would accept the invitation and he drinks beer. Readers regularly tell him that he changed their life. Pretty sure I made a similar claim when sending him that e-mail. But I have proof. I just finished writing a book that never would have happened without this admiration.

Viktor Frankl helped me realize the magnitude of our ability to make choices. He authored *Man's Search for Meaning*, in addition to many other highly recommended books. As a Nazi concentration camp survivor, he often described his experiences and the psychotherapeutic methods developed under those nightmarish conditions. He was a brilliant man who perhaps articulated the most empowering message that has ever been stated.

Do I dare paraphrase such a profound literary piece? Better to beg for forgiveness, right? Dr. Frankl basically said, "Sometimes things suck. But we get to pick our reaction to the suckiness that gets dealt to us." He formulated ideologies equipping people, myself included, to take ownership and responsibility for the choices they make, including emotions in the toughest of circumstances. Even when terrible things are done to us, we aren't forced to view ourselves as victims. Nothing and no one can make us feel or do anything. Here's the quote I think everyone needs to read, digest, and strive to exemplify:

"Between stimulus and response, there is a space. In that space lies our freedom and power to choose our response. In our response lies our growth and freedom."

This quote was the desktop background on my computer for more years than I can remember because I wanted to see it every day, over and over, with the goal of engraining it in my soul. And that absolutely happened. I finally replaced the quote on my computer, by the way. It's not quite as profound, especially considering the context, but still is one I think is worthy of promoting. This was said by Lester Bangs, played by Philip Seymour Hoffman, in the movie *Almost Famous*:

"The only true currency in this bankrupt world is what you share with someone else when you're uncool."

I'm not sure how I feel about that quote swap, in hindsight. But I hear Viktor Frankl talking to me every single day.

Mike Petrusky helped me gain the confidence to say what I have to say. He's the first person in this group with whom I have a nonimaginary relationship, and I'm thrilled to be able to give him a shout-out as a colleague and a friend. Mike hosts several podcasts and is very, very talented at his craft of engaging people in conversations to create valuable content.

I have long felt there were ideas and concepts smoldering upstairs in the belfry that could potentially help people outside my current sphere. This is the I-have-something-to-say spiel. Without Mike, I might never have realized that *anyone else* actually cared what I had to say. Mike showed a confidence that other people could benefit from hearing my thoughts. He believed in me and also made an investment by extending invitations to appear as a guest on his podcast multiple times. He took a chance on a loudmouth, and I appreciate his loyalty. The idea for "So what?" as a stand-alone topic was born on one of the podcasts we did together. These experiences showed me that it wasn't ridiculous to think I possessed some wares that could be put to work by invigorating my WHY.

After all, I'm a guy who cleans floors for a living, always proudly passionate about taking care of our customers and our employees. But who would pay attention to, much less learn anything from, my thoughts about grander-scale ideas such as helping people get to a better place? For some reason, Mike felt I had ideas other people might find useful. He gave me a platform. And, like I said, he did it repeatedly. What's the definition of insanity? As the realization hit that others were enjoying takeaways from the concepts we discussed during those broadcasts, I racked up some confidence.

One last time for good cause...if you have something meaningful to say, say it. I encourage anyone with a compelling message to put it out there and not worry about who's listening. With the right intentions, you might be surprised who gravitates in your direction. I hope you find a Mike. Bam! Another pun landed!

Chip Rankin helped me fulfill one of my greatest ambitions. A life goal of mine was to become a small business owner. Because of Chip, I was able to check this off the list. But there's more to the story...much more.

It's one thing to start a business at a young age when you don't have much to lose. It's an entirely different, and risky, proposition when you already have an established career and family to support. But that's where I found myself as a thirtysomething. How could I possibly leave Corporate America and roll the dice on my future by becoming an entrepreneur? Normally, a gamble like this would have winning odds equivalent to the likelihood of changing the tire on a moving car. But normal circumstances don't involve Chip Rankin. Through his vision and ability to see the world in a manner that most people simply cannot, he found a way for us to become partners in his company. Pulling off this feat was an extremely rare win-win-win (his family, my family, and our company) but, as I write these words, we are in the middle of doing just that. So far, so good (do you hear me knocking on wood?).

Of all the roles I have played during my career, being a business owner has generated the highest amount of significant learnings. And the experiences during this time have been the most rewarding, without question. But his influence on me goes much deeper. They say that business and friendship don't mix. Chip and I take pride in blowing that paradigm out of the water. I do understand why this is a commonly held belief and probably true 999 times out of 1,000. However, when it's done properly, the end result is beyond special. We have built a relationship around trust that shows how everything I have explained throughout the book about these situational decisions are more than just words. We put trust, and the three requisites, into practice every day. This partnership we have built together, founded in trust, is precious to me. He has been a role model for me in areas that, quite frankly, finding people who do things the right way is like spotting a yeti. Chip is my brother and sharing the same genes wouldn't make that statement any truer.

Gary M. Krebs helped me become an author. He is a book producer, coach, author, and someone I have grown to admire very much in a relatively short period of time. Before meeting Gary, I was just a guy who wanted so badly to put a bunch of stuff out there (the stuff that really matters?) without the slightest clue how to do it. At the time of our first conversation, I was superearly in the writing process. He encouraged me to keep going. As the result of his vote of confidence, I dedicated many months to typing out everything in my head during the wee hours of the morning and any spare minute I could find at night, weekends, and even vacations. I don't paint or play an instrument. And I barely golf. Writing became an unexpectedly wonderful new passion for me. Eventually, the first draft of a manuscript was completed, but it wasn't a "book." I don't know exactly what it was. I just know it wasn't something readable for anyone else. Experts were needed to make that happen. Fortunately, they entered my life. That's where his company, GMK Writing and Editing, Inc., got involved in a big way.

Gary put together a team of highly skilled professionals who accomplished the impossible. Their knowledge, experience, and patience turned my jumbled thoughts into a published book, and me into an author. The newfound mantra of mine—if you have something meaningful to say, you should say it—became a flurry of intoxicating activity. Here is the posse that made it happen:

- **Randy Ladenheim-Gil:** Copyediting and proofreading

- **Libby Kingsbury:** Cover design, cover layout, interior design, and interior layout

- **Alesha Peluso:** Marketing and coaching services

- **Joan Shapiro:** Indexer

Nothing I could say would do justice to what I want these individuals to know. But I am saying them anyway because, well, I think that's what you do in this section. After putting up with my not knowing anything about their industry, more questions than bargained for, and way too many out-there ideas, they deserve a medal. I highly recommend each of these individuals in their areas of expertise and urge anyone out there who thinks they have a book in them to contact Gary and get those wheels in motion.

Noel Hudson helped me learn so much about the reasons people do what they do. He has taught me more about the way relationships work than I ever thought possible. In 1996, I was registered for my first-ever sales training course. Fast forward years later and I have a few thousand more of those sessions under my belt, so it seems, and counting. Anyway, I was excited to learn about "sales" and to begin a new career path as a young, enterprising professional. I rolled into the classroom sporting a brand-new suit and tie. The instructor was Noel Hudson. Several days later, at the conclusion of our workshop, I was a changed person. Yes, Noel shared innovative information with me and the other students about the sales process. These were gifts to drive effectiveness. His sagacity about why people buy is unequaled, but what I really learned from him during those days, and every day since, went beyond selling. My views on how relationships are initiated, built, and cultivated were fundamentally reconstructed forever.

A few decades later, I would struggle to mention anyone who has been directly involved with more game-changing lessons learned than Noel Hudson. He has been a coach, a mentor, and a friend. I am fortunate in many ways that our paths crossed at what now seems like a serendipitous moment. Not only would my career, and this book, have been lesser without his teachings, but I can thankfully say the same about my life.

Each of you has helped make the world a better place. I can only hope with all my heart that someday, somehow, someway, there is a somebody out there who says the same thing about me. That's the most superlative, and disruptive, compliment I could ever receive.

SUGGESTED READING

Start with Why: How Great Leaders Inspire Everyone to Take Action, Simon Sinek (Portfolio, 2011)
Including The Golden Circle
https://www.youtube.com/watch?v=qp0HIF3Sfl4

Find Your Why: A Practical Guide for Discovering Purpose for You and Your Team, Simon Sinek, David Mead, Peter Docker (Portfolio, 2017)

Who Moved My Cheese? An Amazing Way to Deal with Change in Your Work and in Your Life, Spencer Johnson (Vermilion, 1999)

The Subtle Art of Not Giving a F*ck: A Counterintuitive Approach to Living a Good Life, Mark Manson (Harper, 2016)
Including the "Do Something" Principle
https://markmanson.net/how-to-get-motivated

Everything Is F*cked: A Book About Hope, Mark Manson (Harper, 2019)

"The Three Levels of Self-Awareness," Mark Manson (markmanson.net/self-awareness)

Man's Search for Meaning, Viktor Frankl (Beacon Press, 2000)

And for good measure, I highly recommend typing the following keyword combinations listed in the order of appearance in this book into any search engine. But you have been warned. Get ready to enter an abyss. You will learn a lot and be entertained by some great reads. Just be prepared to not get much done on your list of chores:

illusory truth effect
confirmation bias
iPod history
Voltaire quotes
difference between hearing and listening
Robert Evans three sides to every story
motivation and motives not the same
communication styles
history of s'mores
cognitive biases
Newton's first law of motion
Phaedrus quotes
rule of 7
empathy sympathy compassion differences
how to become more empathetic
mirror neurons
platinum rule tony alessandra
reading versus watching tv
need more critical thinking
Billy Joel awesome

INDEX

Page numbers in *italics* refer to figures. Entries followed by (QTM #__) refer to individual Questions That Matter. absolutes, 106–107

ABOUT THE AUTHOR: GEOFF SNAVELY

Photo © Maureen Porto Photography

Perhaps more than you want to know…
For many authors, writing a book represents the culmination of their experiences. For Geoff Snavely, the journey has been a long and winding road—and it's just getting started. You see, he lives and breathes Disruptive Discovery every day and doesn't plan on stopping. In fact, he is in the middle of an epic road trip and this book represents his way of picking up as many hitchhikers as possible to come along for the ride. The irony, as he likes to quickly remind people, is that…well…he isn't a writer. At least, not in the traditional sense.

Geoff has carved out a career as a business professional, first and foremost. A proven leader in various roles, an entrepreneur, and part-owner of EBC Carpet Services, a commercial floor and textile care company. The first dozen or so years after college were spent working for large companies in Corporate America. After building a strong foundation through those occupational experiences, completing copious training programs, and also earning a Master of Arts in Organization Development, he fulfilled the dream of becoming a small business owner by partnering with one of his closest friends. The path so far has been filled with rewarding adventures, and the fire is raging to create even better such happenings

This aspiring thinker is impassioned by the idea of doing his part to leave the world a better place than he found it. That means waking up every day trying to make a positive difference in the lives of people, so they feel motivated to become the best possible versions of themselves. This is done through achieving a deep understanding of situations and then helping others solve their unique problems or support their specific needs. With that in mind, he strives to *only* focus on those things that are meaningful and impactful.

Many years ago, an epiphany occurred around his affinity for asking questions and embracing the power of discovery. More specifically, he came to a compelling realization:

Understanding why people do what they do = Good to know.

People understanding *themselves* and why *they do what they do* = Welcome to the new world.

Decades of observation, listening to problems, making lots of his own mistakes, learning from them, and benefiting from nuggets gleaned from several incredible mentors have put him in a position to pass along insights that can possibly do some good for individuals and groups in their different circles—professional, personal, or both. Snavely sincerely believes that if someone has something compelling to say—something that could make an impact—they should say it…so he did. Now, "newbie author" can be checked off the list.

Working life takes up a big chunk of his heart, but most of it has already been captured. Geoff lives in Annapolis, MD, with his Wife (Katharene) and two Daughters (Ella and Alex). They are the three true loves of his life. In addition to his company, he is also a property investor, with houses in Lewes, DE, and the Deep Creek Lake area in Western MD. He bleeds Midnight Green during football season pulling for his beloved Philadelphia Eagles, spends way too much time binge-watching TV, and is often accused of having really bad taste in music.

Disruptive Discovery is an experienced-based facilitation model involving a heavy emphasis on "The 10 Questions That Matter." The mission of this first book is to create a community of disruptors—Facilitators of Betterment—and energize them to make their own positive difference in the lives of others by focusing on what really matters, not wasting time on the stuff that, you know, doesn't. It's a vehicle to share what's on his mind in an attempt to help people help other people. Will it work? Will it be a difference-maker? He hopes so and is issuing a challenge to find out. Better yet, *to get disruptive.*

Are you ready to join him?

Visit Geoff Snavely at disruptivediscovery.com

You can also contact Geoff directly by emailing him at geoff@disruptivediscovery.com

CPSIA information can be obtained
at www.ICGtesting.com
Printed in the USA
LVHW010708151021
700520LV00008B/175

9 781737 957102